T0368526

THE PURSUIT OF Holiness

BY

DOROTHY PRINCEWILL

© 2025 Dorothy Princewill. All rights reserved.

No part of this book may be reproduced, stored in a retrieval system, or
transmitted by any means without the written permission of the author.

AuthorHouse™
1663 Liberty Drive
Bloomington, IN 47403
www.authorhouse.com
Phone: 833-262-8899

Because of the dynamic nature of the Internet, any web addresses or links contained in this book may have changed
since publication and may no longer be valid. The views expressed in this work are solely those of the author and do not
necessarily reflect the views of the publisher, and the publisher hereby disclaims any responsibility for them.

Any people depicted in stock imagery provided by Getty Images are models,
and such images are being used for illustrative purposes only.
Certain stock imagery © Getty Images.

This book is printed on acid-free paper.

Unless otherwise indicated, Bible quotations are from the HOLY SCRIPTURE.
Scripture marked KJV and NKJV are taken from King James and New King James Version. Copyright in 1982 by Thomas
Nelson, Inc. Used by permission. All rights reserved. Scriptures marked NLT are taken from New Living Translation.
Copyright in 1996 by Tyndale House Publishers, Inc. Wheaton, Illinois. Used by permission. All rights reserved.

ISBN: 979-8-8230-3305-3 (sc)
ISBN: 979-8-8230-3306-0 (e)

Print information available on the last page.

Published by AuthorHouse 02/03/2025

authorHOUSE®

TABLE OF CONTENTS

DEDICATION

THIS BOOK IS DEDICATED TO GOD ALMIGHTY, THE HOLY ONE OF ISREAL. THE CREATOR OF THE WHOLE UNIVERSE, THE REVEALER OF SECRET THINGS, ALL KNOWING GOD.

TO THE LORD JESUS CHRIST THE SON OF THE HIGHEST GOD, OUR EMMANUEL, OUR REDEEMER, OUR COMFORTER, COUNCELOR, THE LION OF TRIBE OF JUDA, THE LORD OF SABOAT, THE PRINCE OF PEACE, THE SOON COMING KING.

TO THE HOLY SPIRIT OF GOD OUR COMFORTER, OUR DIRECTOR, OUR CHIEF EXECUTIVE OFFICER (CEO), OUR LEADER, AND OUR MANAGER.

ACKNOWLEDGMENTS

Primarily, I want to give GOD all the glory and honor for this revelation HE gave to me in my study room one morning few years ago. **"NOT PURSUIT OF HAPPINESS BUT PURSUIT OF HOLINESS."** This book is all about the words I heard from the LORD HIMSELF. The Scripture confirmed this in 1st Peter 1:15-17. I am grateful to you LORD, for your grace and your mercy. It is your grace and mercy that has brought me so far in authoring this book.

15 But now you must be holy in everything you do, just as God who chose you is holy. 16 For the Scriptures say, "You must be holy because I am holy."

17 And remember that the heavenly Father to whom you pray has no favorites. He will judge or reward you according to what you do. So, you must live in reverent fear of him during your time here as "temporary residents." (1st Peter 1:15-17 NLT).

I also want to express my gratitude to my husband who encouraged me to do what GOD has asked me to do in putting this book together. His contribution is highly appreciated. I will not fail to mention Women of Divine Purpose for their prayers and support during this time. I want to thank Wailing Women 7 A.M. watch. Thank you for your prayers and care for me.

INTRODUCTION

The whole world is turning or has turned upside-down. A lot of things are happening that this generation never thought in their wildest imagination would happen. So, for Christians, is this a wonderful time to be alive or is a horrible time to be alive? The Bible warned us that on the last days perilous time will come. Are we at that time now or are we expecting a perilous time still? Today, there is nothing like holiness. GOD created HEAVEN and earth. HE is the founder of the whole universe. Genesis chapter one verse one made it clear that in the beginning GOD created the HEAVEN and the earth. There is confusion all over the world. Man that GOD created in HIS image has broken every ordinances of GOD HIS maker. The issue of iniquity or sin depicts the Bible. There are at least eight different terms in the Hebrew Old Testament reflecting some aspect of sin, e.g., "iniquity," "bad," "wickedness," "unrighteousness" etc. Approximately thirteen diverse words in the New Testament of the Bible also portray numerous shades of iniquity, e.g., "evil," "unrighteousness," "transgression," etc.

Iniquity has left a deadly inheritance upon our earth and its inhabitants as we shall prove. It must be noted initially, however, that "sin" does not exist in emptiness. Lucifer was the first sinner (1 John 3:8; cf. John 8:44), and he deceived our original parents (Genesis 3:6-8). Moreover, death became the common epidemic of all biological life (Genesis 2:17; Romans 5:12; 6:23). Because of human rebellion, the entire "creation" was subjected to the "bondage of corruption" (Romans 8:20-21). As I mentioned earlier on, there was the first consequence of the sin that plagued the newly created earth. It is scarcely understood, however, what a disastrous effect the Flood of Noah's day had upon our planet.

Today evil is preferred over righteousness. We welcome atrocities and rebuke what is good and what was normal in the past. What happened to be holy because I AM HOLY? Even among so-called Christians. We are at the end of time. Some who call themselves pastors preach heresy. During preaching, the name of JESUS CHRIST of Nazareth is not mentioned. Many go into the ministry with a wrong motive. Money has become the goal of going into the ministry and opening a church. I am not condemning anyone who is a Minister of GOD. But when preaching, if preaching the Gospel is no longer the focus then we have a problem. What happened to the Great Commission? This was specific instructions.

"The grass withers and the flowers fade,
But the word of our GOD stands forever."
(ISAIAH 40:8)

that JESUS CHRIST gave in the Book of Matthew 28:19-20 "Go ye therefore, and teach all nations, baptizing them in the name of the Father, and of the Son, and of the Holy Ghost: 20 Teaching them to observe all things whatsoever I have commanded you: and, lo, I am with you always, even unto the end of the world" (Matthew 28:19-20).

In some part of Africa, there are a lot of competitions among men and women of GOD, who will have the highest members because the more members that they have the more money that will be contributed to the Church. Some even go as far as looking for demonic powers to perform miracles to attract people who are desperate for GOD'S help. They take advantage of helpless members who need help from GOD. They made themselves GOD. Ministers of GOD I am not judging anyone, but you know yourself. It is either you repent, or you will be exposed, and eternal shame will be your part. You cannot mislead the flocks that GOD trusted in your care. Some of you go to water spirit to buy power thereby defiling the people of GOD.

If you do not repent, the gate of hell is waiting for you soon. You will also give account to GOD for the people you deceived. STOP HAVING SEXUAL INTERCOURSE WITH WATER SPIRIT. I pray that you come openly and confessed your sins so that GOD will forgive you. In HIS anger HE will always remember HIS mercy. Friends there are still time to repent and turn from your evil ways and come back to GOD HE will forgive and make you whole again. In 1st John 1: 8-10 it is clearly said that "If we claim we have no sin, we are only fooling ourselves and not living in the truth. But if we confess our sins to HIM, HE is faithful and just forgives our sins and cleanses us of all wickedness. If we claim we have not sinned, we are calling GOD a liar and showing that HIS word has no place in our hearts." (NLT). Let us seek the mercy of GOD while HE may be found because time is coming when all doors of repentance will be closed just like the door of Noah's Ark. Before the beginning of time, the grace of JESUS CHRIST was made available to us. It was when CHRIST saved us that HE called each one of us to holiness.

**"The grass withers and the flowers fade,
But the word of our GOD stands forever."
(ISAIAH 40:8)**

CHAPTER 1

EVENT AT GARDEN OF EDEN

Deception in the Garden of Eden leads to eternal damnation Lucifer. Adam and Eve plus sin equals to death. JESUS CHRIST death on the Cross equals to everlasting life. As in Adam all die, so in the LORD JESUS CHRIST shall all be made alive. The first Adam and the second Adam here stand as the heads of Humankind. We inherited from Adam; all that is fleshly in our nature. As true children of GOD, we must die daily in the flesh. We inherit from CHRIST all that is spiritual in our nature; it is immortal, that is growing daily, will finally be raised with a spiritual and immortal body. It is important to know and understand that the association with CHRIST to humanity should not only be dated from the incarnation. CHRIST stood in the same national relation to all who went before as HE does to everyone who has come ever since. "For as in Adam all die, even so in Christ shall all be made alive." (1ˢᵗ Corinthians 15:22).

How Sin Began

Seeing that sin is so terrible and destructive that we need a SAVIOR to compensate us, just how did sin begin? The archangel Lucifer, since known as Satan, was the first to sin against GOD, the first to break HIS laws (Read Ezekiel 28:15-16). Ironically, Satan has since influenced the world to think that humankind was the first to sin. Adam and his wife Eve did sin, but they were not the first to sin. Satan had already rebelled against GOD and was waiting there in the Garden of Eden to plant his lies in their thinking (John 8:42-44). Eve and Adam were the first human beings to sin against GOD, and since then all human beings have sinned in like manner (Romans 5:12). Most people find it problematic to admit sin; they just act as if it did not exist. Nonetheless sin is destructive. If GOD had not provided us with an answer, it would destroy all humankind.

The consequences of CHRIST'S death are co-extensive with the outcomes of Adam's fall-they extend to all men. Nevertheless, the individual accountability depends on and rests with each person as to which he or she will appreciate that which he/she derives from JESUS CHRIST or that which he/she originates from Adam the "OFFENCE" of Adam or the "GRACE" of JESUS CHRIST. Most of the time, the eyes of flesh will take us to hell if we are careless supporting and keeping all that GOD wants us to do about HIS commandments.

Lucifer deceived Eve. Lucifer is the father of all lies. Please abstain from all the devices of the devil. He wants to take many people to go to hell. Hell is not meant for man that GOD created in HIS OWN IMAGE. Hell is for the devil and his agents. Look at the picture below the fruit is so beautiful in the eyes but because it leads to death and that was why GOD instructed Adam and Eve to stay away from it. But the devil deceived them both. Even today, the devil is still misleading many. The Devil has a deceptive spirit that lures people to sin.

And they were both naked, the man and his wife, and were not ashamed. Adam and his lovely wife were enjoying the presence of God having fellowship daily with their maker until the serpent came lied and deceived the woman. At this point, fellowship with GOD and holiness was broken. The fellowship with GOD stopped. It is only sin that separates man from his GOD. Sin came into the world because of the serpent deceiving Eve, the wife of Adam. "For as by one man's disobedience many were made sinners, so also by one Man's obedience many will be made righteous." (Romans 5: 19). Jesus is the good Shepherd who left his throne in heaven and came down to bring us back to God. "For Christ also suffered once for sins, the righteous for the unrighteous, to bring you to God. He was put to death in the body but made alive in the Spirit." (1ˢᵗ Peter 3:18).

Loss of the eyes

"The grass withers and the flowers fade,
But the word of our GOD stands forever."
(ISAIAH 40:8)

All that glitters is not gold. All that attracts our physical eyes will chase us away from the beautiful garden that GOD prepared for HIS Creation. Do not allow things of this world to distract you from obeying GOD'S commandments. Eve saw the beautiful fruit but forgot to remember that it is a forbidden fruit which will eventually lead to death. Satan deceived her by lying to her that she will be wise like GOD if she eats the fruit; and as a direct result her believing the lies of the Lucifer she and her husband Adam lost the divine fellowship with GOD. They were both chased out of Garden of Eden and death followed them. Because of GOD'S own kindness and mercy, HE released HIS SINLESS AND HOLY SON JESUS CHRIST TO REDEEM MAN FROM ETERNAL DAM NATION AND DESTRUCTION THANK YOU OMNIPOTENT, OMNISCIENCE, and OMNIPRESENT GOD FOR YOUR LOVE AND KINDNESS. Adam and Eve, the first man and woman created by GOD as told in the Old Testament BOOK OF GENESIS, are the DADDY and MAMA of all HUMANKIND. Through their deliberate disobedience to the COMMAND OF GOD, sin came into the world.

"The grass withers and the flowers fade,
But the word of our GOD stands forever."
(ISAIAH 40:8)

Who Is Responsible for Original Sin---Eve Or Adam?

The Original explanation of the fall specifies that it was Eve who ate the fruit first. Throughout history, numerous people have been led even in our current times to believe that Eve was the person responsible for original sin. We have heard the old fable, "we would not be in this chaos (meaning the overall sinfulness of our tumbled world) would not been possible if it was not for the woman." Nevertheless, is this a true statement? Is Eve to blame for the original sin? There is no doubt that the serpent deceived her. But it was Adam that GOD gave this instruction not to eat the fruit in the middle of the Garden of Eden not Eve.

According to the Book of Genesis, "So when the woman saw that the tree was good for food, that it was pleasant to the eyes, and a tree desirable to make one wise, she took of its fruit and ate. She also gave it to her husband with her, and he ate" (Genesis 3:6). The preceding verse makes us understand that our mother Eve was the first to eat from the tree of knowledge of good and evil. God had told Adam not to eat from the tree, but Eve also had knowledge of this (Genesis 3:2–3). Adam ate but only after Eve. From this account, it is clear for us to conclude that Eve is indeed to be blamed for original sins since she sinned first. Eve was deceived and Adam was not. It is important to bear in mind that this specific instruction was given to Adam.

Just as sin and death came through one man, Adam, it is also through one man, Jesus Christ, that grace and righteousness are given as free gifts to sinners. The naming of Christ as the Last Adam and the multiple comparisons of Adam to Christ would be invalid and nonsensical if original sin came through Eve. Interestingly, although Eve was the first to sin, the solution to sin came through "her Seed" (Genesis 3:15). The Seed, Jesus Christ, was born of a virgin named Mary. He paid the price for sin and will redeem those who receive the salvation He offers. For since by man came death, by Man also came the resurrection of the dead. For as in Adam all die, even so in Christ all shall be made alive.

In the book of Roman 5:12-21 "12 When Adam sinned, sin entered the world. Adam's sin brought death, so death spread to everyone, for everyone sinned. 13 Yes, people sinned even before the law was passed. But it was not counted as a sin because there was not yet any law to break. 14 Still, everyone died—from the time of Adam to the time of Moses—even those who obeyed an explicit commandment of God, as Adam did. Now Adam is a symbol, a representation of Christ, who was yet to come.

15 But there is a great difference between Adam's sin and God's gracious gift. For the sin of this one man, Adam, brought death to many.

"The grass withers and the flowers fade,
But the word of our GOD stands forever."
(ISAIAH 40:8)

But even greater is God's wonderful grace and his gift of forgiveness to many through this other man, Jesus Christ. 16 And the result of God's gracious gift is very different from the result of that one man's sin. For Adam's sin led to condemnation, but God's gift leads to our being made right with God, even though we are guilty of many sins. 17 For the sin of this one man, Adam, caused death to rule over many. But even greater is God's wonderful grace and his gift of righteousness, for all who receive it will live in triumph over sin and death through this one man, Jesus Christ.

18 Yes, Adam's one sin brings condemnation for everyone, but Christ's one act of righteousness brings a right relationship with God and new life for everyone. 19 Because one-person disobeyed God, many became sinners. But because one other person obeyed God, many will be made righteous.

**"The grass withers and the flowers fade,
But the word of our GOD stands forever."
(ISAIAH 40:8)**

20 God's law was given so that all people could see how sinful they were. But as people sinned increasingly, God's wonderful grace became more abundant. 21 So just as sin ruled over all people and brought them to death, now God's wonderful grace rules instead, giving us right standing with God and resulting in eternal life through Jesus Christ our Lord" (Romans 5:12-21).

What Was the Purpose of Christ's Death?

For people of faith, the death of JESUS was part of a divine strategy to save humanity. The death and resurrection of CHRIST JESUS is at the very heart of the Christian faith. For Christians it is through JESUS'S death that people's broken relationship with GOD is reinstated. This is known as Atonement. JESUS CHRIST death on the cross resulted to eternal life. Adam's failure or disobedience in the Garden of Eden resulted in eternal damnation to humanity. JESUS death on the cross resulted to eternal life for every human being who will accept what HE did for our redemption. The WORD of GOD made it clear about the fact that JESUS had to die for all people of all time and for crucial reasons. HE had to die because of the entire world's sins (yours, mine, and everyone else's). Believers, in most part, if asked what makes them a Christian, would answer like this: I know that JESUS is the SON of GOD and that HE died for my sins, and I accept HIS shed blood for my sins. Even though JESUS did die for us, is that all there is to this belief? Does the WORD of GOD tell us that there is more to the story?

JESUS Sacrifice for Humankind's Sins:

It was sin that brought on JESUS' death. There are several Bible passages that show why JESUS died for humankind. To the believers in Rome, Paul explained: "For all have sinned and

**"The grass withers and the flowers fade,
But the word of our GOD stands forever."
(ISAIAH 40:8)**

fall short of the glory of God, being justified freely by His grace through the redemption that is in Christ Jesus, whom God set forth as a propitiation [atoning sacrifice] by HIS blood, through faith, to demonstrate His righteousness, because in His forbearance God had passed over the sins that were previously committed" (Romans 3:23-25). Apostle Paul wrote that we are to "walk in love, as Christ also has loved us and given Himself for us, an offering and a sacrifice to GOD for a sweet-smelling aroma" (Ephesians 5:2). In the same letter later, the Apostle Paul wrote: "But GOD demonstrates HIS own love toward us, in that while we were still sinners, Christ died for us.

Much more than, having now been justified by HIS blood, we shall be saved from wrath through HIM" (Romans 5:8-9). Paul explained to the church in Corinth that GOD the Father "made HIM who knew no sin [JESUS CHRIST] to be sin for us" (2 Corinthians 5:21). At this point, the clear insinuation is that JESUS took our guilt mine and yours on HIMSELF and paid the ultimate penalty for us by HIS DEATH on the Cross as a criminal. John the beloved also

**"The grass withers and the flowers fade,
But the word of our GOD stands forever."
(ISAIAH 40:8)**

explained the reason for Jesus' death: "If anyone does sin, we have an advocate with the Father, Jesus Christ the righteous; and he is the atoning sacrifice for our sins, and not for ours only but also for the sins of the whole world" (1 John 2:1-2, NRSV).

The WORD of GOD is very clear about the detail that JESUS had to die for all people of all time and for vital reasons. He had to die because of human sin, yours, mine, and everyone else's. The prophet Isaiah documented the purpose of JESUS' death centuries before it happened:" HE was wounded for our transgressions, HE was bruised for our iniquities; the chastisement for our peace was upon HIM, and by HIS stripes we are healed" (Isaiah 53:5). So, with all the sufferings of JESUS on the cross we ought to obey HIM with everything that we have gotten. Brothers and sisters, please do not let the agony of CHRIST on the Cross be against on you on the judgment day. Everyone will give an account of his or her work here on earth. CHRIST loved us so much hence HE agreed to come to die for us to reconcile us to HIS FATHER. It cost HIM HIS LIFE to bring us back to GOD after Adam failed in the Garden of Eden. CHRIST death brought us hope and feature. Let us pursue Holiness and not happiness. Holiness is eternal and happiness is temporal.

God demands us to be holy. In Hebrews (12:14 KJV), we were instructed to follow peace with all men, and holiness, without which no man shall see the LORD. As CHRIST followers we must ask ourselves if we are living our lives in obedience to the command to pursue holiness. Are we walking in obedience to the authoritative word of ALL and MIGHTY GOD?

"The grass withers and the flowers fade,
But the word of our GOD stands forever."
(ISAIAH 40:8)

Are we pursuing holiness, or are we pre-occupied pursuing material things? Is one thing to claim to be a Christian and another thing is really obeying GOD'S will in our life? If we want to be holy like GOD instructed us to be, we must aspire to grow deeper in our relationship with GOD. Christian race is an individual one, and each one of us must give account of themselves. I am sorry to say this, and I am disappointed that even so many Christians including men and women in the ministry, for example Preachers, Bishops, Evangelist, and other servants of GOD today do not preach and emphasis in holiness. To many of us, holiness is outdated. May GOD help us to embrace holiness as we run this race that is set before us?

Even in our pulpits today many preachers are no longer preaching to their audience that there is hell and their Heaven because of the fear of people living in the church. We are more concerned about having a multitude of members than people flooding hell fire. Holiness was broken in the Garden of Eden. Genesis (2:7; 21-25) And the LORD God formed man of the dust of the ground, and breathed into his nostrils the breath of life; and man became a

living soul. And the LORD caused a deep sleep to fall upon Ad'am, and he slept: and he took one of his ribs and closed the flesh instead thereof: And the rib, which the LORD GOD had taken from man, made a woman, and brought her unto the man. And Adam said, This is now bone of my bones, and flesh of my flesh she shall be called Woman, because she was taken out of Man.

For many of us who claimed to be Christians, take inventory of your walk with GOD because we all need to stand before Him and give account of how we lived our life's here on earth. Some of us are hypocrites. Remember the judgement will start in the house of God. Pastors, you are scared to preach holiness so that you will not lose your financial members. You preach prosperity so you can have many carnal members who will lavish you with blood-stained money in offerings and tithes. God is your provider. When He calls you, He will also equip you for the ministry. The LORD has not given us the spirit of fear but of a sound mind to preach the gospel without any form of reservation. 1 Thessalonians (4: 7) For God did not call us to uncleanness, but holiness. The Alter of GOD is broken and defiled in many Churches today.

Social media has so much negative influence on Christians today. As a result of this negative influence, many so-called pastors are now dancing to their tone. What God says that is abomination is now acceptable by many Christians and ordained pastors. Since we are on the last days, there is a call to return to our base. Return to our first love. Return to holiness. Without holiness no man will see God. In the book of Isaiah chapter (45:9-12) it says Woe unto him that striveth with his Maker.

**"The grass withers and the flowers fade,
But the word of our GOD stands forever."
(ISAIAH 40:8)**

Let the potsherd strive with the potsherds of the earth. Shall the clay say to him that fashioned it, What makest thou? Or thy work, He hath no hands? Woe unto him that saith unto his father, What begettest thou? Or to the woman, What hast thou brought forth? Bishops, Evangelists, Pastors, Missionaries, Apostles, and all other Christians the bible made it clear in 2nd Timothy (2:21) If a man therefore purge himself from these, he shall be a vessel unto honour, sanctified, and meet for the master's use, and prepared unto every good work.

So, how can we carry out this commandment when we are full of selfishness and self-centeredness? Brothers and sisters there is hell and there is heaven. Joshua said to the children of

"The grass withers and the flowers fade, But the word of our GOD stands forever." (ISAIAH 40:8)

Israel choose ye this day who you shall serve but as for me and house we will serve the LORD GOD ALMIGHTY. We still have a little time to repent. Remember there is no repentance in the grave. Those of you that called yourselves ministers of God and at the same time doing what is abominable before God; please repent. God is a merciful God. He is willing and ready to forgive you. This writer is not better than you. We have all disappointed God. I believe that if we truly and repent He is a kind God, He will take us back. James (1:21-22). Wherefore, lay apart all filthiness and superfluity of naughtiness, and receive with meekness the engrafted word which can save your souls. But be ye doers of the word, and not hearers only, deceiving your own selves. In (1ˢᵗ John 1:5-10) John clearly writes it the beloved that "This is the message which we have heard from him and announce to you, that God is light, and in him is no darkness at all. 6 If we say that we have fellowship with him and walk in the darkness, we lie, and do not tell the truth. 7 But if we walk in the light, as he is in the light, we have fellowship with one another, and the blood of Jesus Christ, his Son, cleanses us from all sin. 8 If we say that we have no sin, we deceive ourselves, and the truth is not in us. 9 If we confess our sins, he is faithful and righteous to forgive us the sins, and to cleanse us from all unrighteousness. 10 If we say that we have not sinned, we make him a liar, and his word is not in us." How can we say we are Christians when we purposely having fellowship with devil. Doing what God says we should not do. We should not be supportive evil so we can be accepted by people who do not care about keeping the commandments of God.

As a result of disobedient to God, death and all its initial glitches are the consequences of human disobedience to his Creator. When God put Adam in the Garden of Eden, the Lord God Almighty warned Adam that "the day" he ate of the forbidden fruit he would "die." "Death" is used in numerous senses in the Scripture, yet it continuously suggests some kind of separation.

**"The grass withers and the flowers fade,
But the word of our GOD stands forever."
(ISAIAH 40:8)**

When the first family ate of that "fruit" there was an instantaneous separation from their Creator in both spiritual and physical sense. The moment Adam and Eve were banished from the Eden and the "tree of life," Both of them were subjected to a procedure of disintegration which finally would end in physical death (Genesis 3:22-24; 5:5), the separation of the spirit from the body (James 2:26). Every single disease common to human race is the consequence of our remote ancestors' revolt against God. Wherefore, as by one man sin entered the world, and death by sin; and so, death passed upon all men, for that all have sinned (Romans 5:12). Death is regarded as human enemy. The last enemy that shall be destroyed is death (1 Corinthians 15:26). When sickness and death stalk us, we must be reminded of the atrocious nature of evil and endeavor to circumvent such at all costs. Man born of woman is but of few days and full of trouble (Job 14:1).

In summary, GOD'S love is different than normal human love. GOD loves us when we are completely unlovable. When JESUS died, HE died for the ungodly, for sinners, and for HIS enemies. Apostle Paul gets at how conflicting this is to human nature when he writes, "For one will scarcely die for a righteous person, though perhaps for a good person one would dare to die, but God shows HIS love for us in that while we were sinners, CHRIST died for us.

**"The grass withers and the flowers fade,
But the word of our GOD stands forever."
(ISAIAH 40:8)**

(Romans 5:7–8). Certainly, the death of JESUS was real in its purpose. CHRIST goal was not only to buy the possibility of redemption, but a people for HIS own possession. The LORD wrote in John gospel: "All that the Father gives to me will come to me, and whoever comes to me I will never cast out… And this is the will of him who sent me, that I should lose nothing of all that he has given me but raise it up on the last day" (John 6:36, 39). Remember that a day of reckoning is coming, be ready to give an account of your life. It is imperative for all believes to do a self-reflection daily in our walk with GOD.

**"The grass withers and the flowers fade,
But the word of our GOD stands forever."
(ISAIAH 40:8)**

CHAPTER 2

THE DEATH OF JESUS CHRIST

JESUS DIED on The Cross for Our Sins:

Why did GOD send HIS ONLY SON TO COME TO THIS WORLD TO REDEEM US? By one man sin came into this world; and by one HOLY SON OF GOD JESUS CHRIST OUR LORD Redemption came. "Who gave Himself as a sacrifice to atone for our sins to save and sanctify us so that HE might rescue us from this present evil age, in accordance with the will and purpose and plan of OUR GOD AND FATHER" (Galatians 1:4 Amplified Bible). The first and most important fact of the gospel Paul preached was that "Christ died for our sins" (1 Cor. 15:3). The reality and purpose of His death are said clearly over and over in Paul's epistles. The most basic fact of the gospel is CHRIST'S death for our sins. The fact is that people died every day. When Adam and Eve sinned in the Garden of Eden, death becomes inevitable for humankind. Remember, GOD told Adam and Eve not to touch the fruit at the center of the Garden if they do, they will die. God set a boundary in the Garden.

Unfortunately, that boundary was crossed and because of deliberate disobedience to GOD'S instructions, death came into the world. In fact, every person who has ever lived has died or will die, with just a few exceptions. Many were also crucified. On the day CHRIST died on the cross, two other men were crucified, one on each side of HIM. What, then, is significant about the death of Christ? Simply, it is that He died for our sins. We call this concept "substitutionary atonement." Christ died instead of us. He did not die for Himself; He died in our place, as our substitute, to atone for our sins and allow us to enter a right relationship with a holy God. The death of Christ as our substitute is the heart of the gospel. It is not just that He died, but that He died for our sins. We call this idea "substitutionary atonement." CHRIST died as an alternative for us. HE did not die for HIMSELF; HE died in our place, as our substitute, to make up for our sins and allow us to enter a right relationship with a HOLY GOD.

JESUS died of a broken heart. My sin alone was more than enough to weigh HIM down. The sins of the whole universe were upon HIM. HE did not deserve this but because of the love HE still went ahead to carry the burdens of everyone. HE paid the debt that HE did not owe, and I owe the debt I could not pay. Who could have done this for us? Only JESUS: Such love that the SAVIOUR should die for sinner such as I. Because of the size of love of GOD for humankind, even when JESUS was praying; "Father, if thou be willing, remove this cup from me: nevertheless, not my will, but thine, be done." (Luke 22:42). Nevertheless, HIS FATHER still let HIM go through this horrible death to bring man back to HIMSELVE.

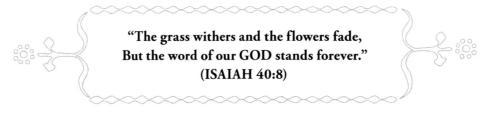

"The grass withers and the flowers fade,
But the word of our GOD stands forever."
(ISAIAH 40:8)

The Prophet Isaiah prophesized in Isaiah 53: 5-8 about what the MESSIAH will go through for humanity. 5 "But he was pierced by our rebellion, crushed for our sins. He was beaten so we could be whole. He was whipped so we could be healed. 6 All of us, like sheep, have strayed away. We have left God's paths to follow our own. Yet the Lord laid on him the sins of us all. 7 He was oppressed and treated harshly, yet he never said a word. He was led like a lamb to slaughter. And as a sheep is silent before the shearers, he did not open his mouth. 8 Unjustly condemned, he was led away. No one cared that he died without descendants, that his life was cut short in midstream. But he was struck down for the rebellion of my people" (Isaiah 53:5–8).

Throughout the history, no man's death likes the death of JESUS CHRIST. The death of JESUS brought eternal hope for man. JESUS death brought hope for human. Through HIS death man was reconciled to HIS MAKER. A Death That Brought Life IT WAS the death of Jesus Christ upon the torture stake over 2,000 years ago. HIS death opened for us a door to life eternal. Without HIS death we would have no hope of regaining the state of sinlessness besides faultlessness in the beginning had by our ancestor Adam. No one of us would have any optimism of seeing the day when death no longer would end every humanoid lifespan. All of us would not have any hope of experiencing an issue from incarceration to death by a resurrection. HIS life as a perfect human was given up as a ransom for everyone.

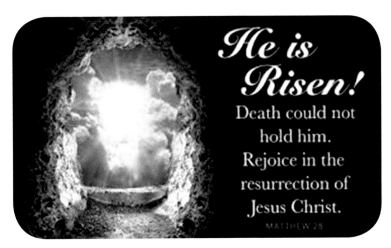

The death of JESUS CHRIST

**"The grass withers and the flowers fade,
But the word of our GOD stands forever."
(ISAIAH 40:8)**

1. Reconciled Us to GOD

The death of JESUS CHRIST brought us SALVATION. It reconciled us to GOD. Validation, propitiation, plus redemption are all benefits of Christ's death and it has one pronounced purpose: reconciliation. JESUS'S death enables us to have a joy-filled association with GOD, which is the uppermost good of the cross. "And you, who once were alienated and hostile in mind, doing evil deeds, HE has now reconciled in his body of flesh by his death, in order to present you holy and blameless and above reproach before him" (Colossians 1:21-22) writes Paul. Without JESUS dying on the cross, there will be no Salvation. It was the sins of the first man and first woman (Adam and Eve) that separated us from our CREATOR. But the death of a sinless man JESUS brought us back to GOD. We came to this world with a sinful nature, and as a result, we are alienated from God. Only forgiveness which was bought at the cross by JESUS can heal the relationship so that we are able to enjoy fellowship with God. What a merciful GOD that we have. For GOD so loved the world, that HE gave HIS only begotten Son, that whosoever believeth in HIM should not perish, but have everlasting life (John 3:16). It is because of that sin that took place in the Garden of Eden that we experience pain and are separated from God. Nevertheless, there is still hope for us and that hope is through Jesus Christ.

God Almighty came down from heaven as a man JESUS CHRIST; lived a flawless life, and then died a blameless death on the cross so that we could live a free and original life with HIM. JESUS offered an opportunity to live a freer life through the forgiveness of our sins on the cross. There is still time to accept this gift of GOD because of the death of JESUS CHRIST on the Calvary. "From that time forth began Jesus to shew unto his disciples, how that he must go to Jerusalem, and suffer many things of the elders, and chief priests and scribes, and be killed, and be raised again the third day. Then Peter took him, and began to rebuke him, saying, "Be it far from thee, Lord: this shall not be unto thee. But he turned, and said unto Peter, Get thee behind me, Satan: thou art an offence unto me: for thou savourest not the things that be of God, but those that be of men" (Matt. 16:21–23).

2. Outlines what Love is for us

CHRIST'S death was not just an act of love, it *describes* love. HIS death is the ultimate example of what love ought to be, and Jesus calls those who follow him to walk in the same kind of life-laying-down love. According to what John wrote in (1st John 3:16), "By this we know love, that he laid down his life for us, and we ought to lay down our lives for the brothers. But if anyone has the world's goods and sees his brother in need, yet closes his heart against him, how does God's love abide in him? Little children, let us not love in word or talk but indeed and in truth."

"The grass withers and the flowers fade,
But the word of our GOD stands forever."
(ISAIAH 40:8)

3. To Save and Redeem Us from Eternal Condemnation

JESUS'S death was substitutionary. This means that HE died in our place. We deserved the death that HE died. HE bore the punishment that was rightly ours. For everyone who believes in HIM, CHRIST took the wrath of GOD on our behalf. Peter writes, "JESUS HIMSELF bore our sin in his body on the tree that we might die to sin and live to righteousness. By HIS wounds you have been healed" (1ST Peter 2:24). God's love is different from human love. God loves us when we are completely unlovable. When JESUS died, HE died for the ungodly, for sinners, and for his enemies. Paul gets at how contrary this is to human nature when he writes, "For one will scarcely die for a righteous person, though perhaps for a good person one would dare to die, but God shows his love for us in that while we were sinners, Christ died for us" (Romans 5:7-8).

The summary of the whole matter is that all of us have sinned and deserve GOD'S judgment. GOD, the ALL and MIGHTY FATHER, sent HIS only SON to satisfy that judgment for those who believe in HM. JESUS CHRIST, the CREATOR and ETERNAL SON OF GOD, who lived a sinless life, loves us so much that HE died for our sins, taking the chastisement that we deserve, was buried, and rose from the dead according to the Bible, If you truly believe and belief this in your heart, accepting JESUS alone as your Savior, proclaiming, "JESUS IS LORD"," you will be saved from decree and spend eternity with GOD in heaven, our final destination. "Let not your heart be troubled: ye believe in God, believe also in me. In my Father's house are many mansions: if it were not so, I would have told you. I will go to prepare a place for you. And if I go and prepare a place for you, I will come again and receive you unto myself; that where I am, there ye may be also" (John 14:1-3).

Surrender your life today to JESUS CHRIST. Tomorrow might be too late for you. There is no repentance in the grave. Today is your day; so, maximize the moment with JESUS CHRIST YOUR SAVIOR. HE loves you so much. He saved me and HE is willing to save you and make you a new creature in HIM.

**"The grass withers and the flowers fade,
But the word of our GOD stands forever."
(ISAIAH 40:8)**

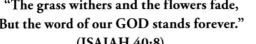

"The grass withers and the flowers fade,
But the word of our GOD stands forever."
(ISAIAH 40:8)

CHAPTER 3

WHO IS ON THE LORD SIDE?

Currently, it is hard to see people who will stand for the LORD in the society that we are living in today. Many have gone their own ways. People do not even believe the existence of GOD not to talk about standing for HIM. In the book of Exodus 32:26 – "Then Moses stood in the gate of the camp, and said, Who is on the Lord 's side? let him come unto me. And all the sons of Levi gathered themselves together with him. Dear brothers and sisters, looking at the question that Moses asked the nation of Israel in the wilderness as he stood in the gate of the camp after he returned from the mount to find that Israel had made a golden calf and started worshiping it and committing all kinds of idolatry and sin. Moses had talked to God and received the law, the Ten Commandments, but he returned to find the children of Israel just as we are found before the law, all of us are all guilty, we all have broken and break GOD'S law. Many people were killed that day after Moses came back and dealt with them, and that is a picture of bringing of the law. We are not better than the children of Israel who broke GOD'S heart upon the return of Moses. I wonder if CHRIST should come back today how many of us are ready to go with HIM.

I call these generation GOD haters. So many atrocities are being committed today, things that we never heard of in the past have now been accepted as the norm. Now, dear friends, as Moses did, on that occasion, needs to be done very frequently in our current generation. It is needful that a banner should be exhibited because of the truth, and that men should be called out, to rally around it; and those, who do so, those who are the most courageous and the most faithful, shall obtain a great reward, even as it is written in the Book of Deuteronomy, that Moses gave a special blessing upon the tribe of Levi because its sons were faithful in that trying and challenging time: "And of Levi he said, Let thy Thummim and thy Urim be with thy holy one, whom thou didst prove at Massah, and with whom thou didst strive at the waters of Meribah; who said unto his father and to his mother, I have not seen him; neither did he acknowledge his brethren, nor knew his own children: for they have observed thy word, and kept thy covenant." Blessed are they also, who, in these days and age, bow not down before the contemporary idols that so many worship, blessed are the brave men who never question whether a certain progress will "pay" or not, but who do the correct thing, whatsoever the penalties of their action might be.

GOD is faithful. HE is a promise keeper. HE is a covenant keeping GOD. When HE promises HE will surely bring it to pass. JEHOVAH is not a man to tell a lie. If GOD did not

> **"The grass withers and the flowers fade,**
> **But the word of our GOD stands forever."**
> **(ISAIAH 40:8)**

spare Moses from his anger by striking the rock instead of speaking according to GOD's own instructions by not entering the promise land? Do we think that GOD will accept us into heaven when we refused to do what we ought to do? "Now, when Moses saw that the people were out of control--for Aaron had let them get out of control to be derision among their enemies. Then Moses stood in the gate of the camp, and said, "Whoever is for the LORD, come to me!" And all the sons of Levi gathered for him. He said to them, "Thus says the LORD, the God of Israel, 'Every man of you put his sword upon his thigh and go back and forth from gate to gate in the camp, and kill every man his brother, and every man his friend, and every man his neighbor." (Exodus 32:25-27). In the book of Exodus 32:26 which is the second book of the Bible; it becomes imperative that we should carefully examine the significance of what Moses did here.

He calls the children of Israel to order or a mandate either to be on GOD'S side or not. "Then Moses stood in the gate of the camp, and said, who is on the Lord's side? let him come unto me. And all the sons of Levi gathered themselves together with him. Because of this single act of the tribe of Levi, GOD honored them with Priesthood among the tribes of Israel. This means that everyone will be rewarded by following the GOD who created Heaven and earth. It is true that the Bible said that on the last day's people will do whatsoever pleases them. By the grace of GOD, I have been in the LORD for many years, and I can comfortably testify that it pays to serve the Lord. I am declaring that I am on the LORD'S side. I have come so far to quit trusting and totally depending on the LORD for all my needs.

GOD has done me well. I have no reason not to be on the LORD'S side. If I have breath, I will always be on the LORD'S side. My ultimate aspiration is to live a holy life for the GOD that created the universe. The same call that Moses made to the children of Israel is the same call that is engineering me to author this book on A CALL TO HOLINESS FOR GOD IN THESE LAST DAYS TROUBLED TIME OF.

Christians in the Western World the United States of America first are currently experiencing a wave of anti-CHRIST activities in every area. I will narrow my observation on the US. The gap between what is Christian and what is not Christian is spreading in this nation. GOD is using situations such as the latest US Supreme Court Judges ruling on gay "marriage" becomes a clear indication showing who undoubtedly is on the Lord's side. "And if it seems evil to you to serve the Lord, choose for yourselves this day whom you will

> **"The grass withers and the flowers fade,**
> **But the word of our GOD stands forever."**
> **(ISAIAH 40:8)**

serve, whether the gods which your fathers served that were on the other side of the River, or the gods of the Amorites, in whose land you dwell. But as for me and my house, we will serve the Lord" (Joshua 24:15). This is a personal determination that each one of us will have make either to stay on the LORD side or go with the wind of not honoring and obeying GOD. From the work of GOD, we have seen that there are grave consequences when decided to disobey GOD. We need to take a journey back to Garden of Eden to ask Adam and Eve what happened to them when they decided not to follow through with GOD'S instructions. As children of GOD, aspiring to be holy is not negotiable. Where will you spend eternity if Jesus will appear now? Or if you should die now, will you meet HIM at Heaven's gate? Beloved, JESUS is waiting for you to open the door of your heart for HIM to come in. Heaven is real and hell is real. Choose on whose side you will belong.

As you read this book, if you want to give your life to JESUS, Pray this prayer with me: Dear Lord Jesus, I repent of my sin today. I accept what you did for me on the cross of Calvary. My heart to your LORD. Come into my life and control everything about me. I promise to serve you from this day forward. So, help me GOD IN JESUS MIGHTY NAME AMEN. If you pray this prayer, you are now a BORN-AGAIN CHRISTIAN. CONGRATULATIONS. Your name is now written in the BOOK OF LIFE. Now that you have given your life to CHRIST, find a Bible believing Church to attend regularly. Make yourself known to your Pastor. This is very important. Now, then, you who are on "the Lord's side" wherever you are, as you really believe in JESUS, let me the first to congratulate you in your new life in CHRIST. Indeed, more than that, in the name of JESUS, in whom you believe, I urge and command you to confess your faith in HIM. Do not be ashamed to affirm your convictions; do not try to hide yourselves from your fellow-Christians.

**"The grass withers and the flowers fade,
But the word of our GOD stands forever."
(ISAIAH 40:8)**

CHAPTER 4

CONSTANT FELLOWSHIP WITH GOD

Can a Christian Break Fellowship with GOD?

There are many things that can make us break our fellowship with God. The cares of this world will and has made so many people break their fellowship with their Creator. Honestly, the answer is yes. Adam and Eve in the garden of Eden broke their communion with GOD. Judas Iscariot also broke his fellowship with Christ. When a child of GOD backslides, no longer enjoy fellowship with GOD, at this point, he or she has broken the fellowship between himself/herself and GOD. When an individual removes himself or herself under the covering of the head of the universe, fellowship is broken. Many of us today have broken our fellowship with GOD due to cares and deception from this world. The Bible told us the story of how Adam and Eve were enjoying fellowship with God but what happened? According to scripture GOD comes down in the cool of evening to have fellowship with Adam and Eve his wife but unfortunately that fellowship was broken because of sin. Sin stinks before GOD. The only thing that can cut off our fellowship with GOD is sin.

As we will see in Genesis chapter 3 from verse 1-24, the event that took place as a direct result of sin. Adam and Even was driven out of the beautiful garden because fellowship is broken because sin came in and, fellowshipping with God ended. Some of us Christians today have already out of fellowship with GOD. We can go to church but not live a holy life. No church can save us or take us to heaven only our personal relationship with GOD will be a determining factor if we will make heaven or not. There are spirits of deception hovering around all over the world. Believers should ask GOD to give us a spirit of discernment to be able to find which is which.

"The grass withers and the flowers fade,
But the word of our GOD stands forever."
(ISAIAH 40:8)

Enoch walked with GOD without any blameness. He walked with close fellowship with GOD. This man Enoch was not just God pleaser but he lived his life by faith in the GOD of Heaven and earth. He also lived his life in intimate communion with GOD. He was an honest man. He was a faithful man. He honored GOD with everything he had. Enoch was a holy man. To have fellowship with the holy God, we must not walk in the darkness, but walk in the light. "And Enoch walked with GOD: and he was not; for GOD took him."(Genesis 5:24). To walk with GOD, we are obligated to keep in step with HIM. In the direction of keeping in step with GOD ALMIGHTY, we need to perfect our activities after HIS and keep an eye on the instructions or commandments HE has already made available to all of humanity with. This process points to obeying GOD'S instructions concerning moral behavior. Enoch is a man of faith. He followed GOD'S commandments to the core. Friends if Enoch did me and you can also do it because of what JESUS did for us on the Cross of Calvary.

Constant Fellowship with GOD

We mothers especially when we go to the store with our little children we do not want them to walk away from us. I observe that some tie small rope on the hand of their children so they will not walk away from them. If they do, both the parents and the child will experience panic. All the staff in the store will also be concerned. This is exactly what happens between us and GOD when we walk away from HIM. It is even worst than walking away from GOD. This is nothing but heading towards eternal damnation. Fellowship is the greatest significant thing GOD wants from each one us. HE wants us to come to know HIM to be with HIM to spend time with HIM. Whenever we spend time with GOD we hear from HIM and becomes well knowledgable about HIS will in our life and how to live better as HIS children. Moses spend 40 days in the wilderness hearing from GOD and enjoying HIS presence.

"The grass withers and the flowers fade,
But the word of our GOD stands forever."
(ISAIAH 40:8)

JESUS set an example for us when HE slow down the pace of HIS life to spend time with the FATHER. I believe strongly that JESUS knew the importance of quiet momentswith HIS FATHER. HE often went into the mountains to pray. The more mature we become in our relationship with GOD, the more imperative this noiseless time with GOD becomes. Being alone with GOD every day should be our formost priority. Every one of us need to listen to HIM for comfort and direction in our lives every seconds that we have our breath.

In my personal life, I realize that my quite moment with the LORD every day sets up the tune on how my day will go. If we make fellowship with God a priority, all of the crucial matters in our lives will fall into place. When we focus on GOD HE helps us understand the priorities of everything else. JESUS stated in Matthew chapter 6:33 "But seek ye first the kingdom of GOD, and HIS righteousness; and all theses things shall be added unto you."Matthew 6:33). Notice that JESUS did not say some of these things shall be added unto you but **ALL** shall be added unto you. No man or woman can out do GOD. HE is the ALL AND MIGHT GOD. The truth is that we can all become so pre-occupied with non-valuable activities that we neglect some of the vital things in our Christian race that is critically needed for example:

- Spend time with God alone, in prayer,

- To meet with others in fellowship with God.

- Studying the WORD of GOD and meditating on it

- Walking closely with GOD daily

- Not caring about lost souls

- Living in the flesh as non-believers

The truth is that we can become sidetracked from our GOD given purpose in life. GOD made us for HIS pleasure. It is possible that we seriously consider our physical activities of ministry (it might be true that they are necessary) consequently important that we have little if any time to fellowship with GOD. When we are actively engaged in hectic activity on GOD'S behalf (at least at the time it seems that we are engaged in GOD'S business) we can forget what the LORD JESUS said in Matthew 23:23: "Woe to you, teachers of the law and Pharisees, you hypocrites. You give a tenth of your spices – mint, dill and cummin. But you have neglected the important matters of the law – justice, mercy and faithfulness. You should have practiced the latter, without neglecting the former."(Matthew 23:23). The teachers and Pharisees lived under the precise and rigorous physical standards of the old covenant. Sometimes we read this and jeer at the fault-finding exactness of those people, but Jesus was not jeering. The LORD told them that they should have done what the covenant required of them.

**"The grass withers and the flowers fade,
But the word of our GOD stands forever."
(ISAIAH 40:8)**

(Read Genesis 3:1-24)

Now the serpent was more subtil than any beast of the field which the LORD God had made. And he said unto the woman, Yea, hath God said, Ye shall not eat of every tree of the garden? Brothers and sisters do not be deceived that nothing can break our fellowshipping with God. The truth of the matter is that sin will break our communion with God. In Romans chapter 6:1-4 states that we should not continue in sin. If a child of God continues to live a sinful life, he or she is heading to hell. Some of us say that we are in the day of dispensation or under grace, so we can do anything. "What shall we say then?

Shall we continue in sin, that grace may abound? God forbid. How shall we, that are dead to sin, live any longer there? Know ye not, that so many of us as were baptized into Jesus Christ were baptized into his death? Therefore, we are buried with him by baptism into death: that like as Christ was raised up from the dead by the glory of the Father, even so we also should walk in newness of life" (Romans 6:1-4). "This then is the message which we have heard of him, and declare unto you, that God is light, and in him is no darkness at all.

If we say that we have fellowship with him, and walk in darkness, we lie, and do not the truth: But if we walk in the light, as he is in the light, we have fellowship one with another, and the blood of Jesus Christ his Son cleanseth us from all sin. If we say that we have no sin, we deceive ourselves, and the truth is not in us. If we confess our sins, he is faithful and just forgives us our sins, and to cleanse us from all unrighteousness" (1 John 1:5-10).

Why do we need to confess our sins if all sin was forgiven on the cross? All people are sinners by nature and by practice. At conversion all our sins are forgiven–past, present, and future. Yet even after we become Christians, we still sin and need to confess. This kind of confession is not to gain God's acceptance but to remove the barrier that our sin has put between us and Him. The truth is that sin breaks our fellowship with God. So even though we are redeemed and, on our way, to be with Him forever, we are still in a sinful world giving in to sin. When we come before Him in prayer, we need to confess our sin, so we can have complete fellowship with Him. Bringing our sin before Him makes us think about it and therefore gives us wisdom to remove it from our lives.

God cannot be in darkness and sin is darkness, so we must remove all darkness from our lives before He can have fellowship with us. This does not mean that we must confess every sin before we die so we can be with Him. We are covered by the Blood of Christ and will be with Him if we believe Him. But to have fellowship with Him in this world we need to remove the darkness because God is light and there is no darkness in Him at all. So if we want to be with Him, we need to remove the darkness. And we know that growth only happens in the light. A

> **"The grass withers and the flowers fade,**
> **But the word of our GOD stands forever."**
> **(ISAIAH 40:8)**

plant will not grow without light, and neither will we grow in Christ while in darkness. If His Word has a place in your heart, you will grow by being in His presence because He is Light. Darkness cannot exist in the Light, so confess and remove all darkness so you can have fellowship with Him.

Difference between Religion and Christianity

Christianity is not the same from all other religions. Consequently, Christianity is not a religion. Christianity comes from its root word CHRIST. The origin of the word "CHRIST" is resulting from the Greek word Christos which means "THE ANOINTED ONE BY THE HOLY SPIRIT." Christos is the Greek complement of the Hebrew word MASHIACH meaning MESSIAH or SON OF GOD. The Virgin Mary gave the earthly name JESUS as commanded by the Angel Gabriel found in the New Testament book the gospel of Luke chapter 1 verse 31.The Cross of our LORD JESUS CHRIST OF NAZARET symbolizes a lot of meaningful things in a Christians life: "Make every effort to live in peace with everyone and to be holy; without holiness no one will see the Lord."(Hebrews 12:14). Love, forgiveness, healing, redemption, eternal life, no more condemnation, new birth, freedom from the bondage of sin, new life, grace, mercy etc.

The Cross is the trademark of Christianity.

Apostle Paul's letter to the Church of Corinth documented 1ˢᵗ Corinthians chapter 15:1-4 concerning the resurrection of Jesus Christ sum up what Christianity is all about. Christianity centers on the GOSPEL OF JESUS CHRIST. The Gospel is the English translation of the Greek word euangelion or the "GOOD NEWS." The Gospel states that JESUS CHRIST offered His innocent life to save HIS people (the Christians) from the bondage of sin. HE was buried and was resurrected on the third day to fulfill what GOD has revealed through the Prophet Isaiah. JESUS bore with HIM the sins of the entire world so that they may be righteous in the

**"The grass withers and the flowers fade,
But the word of our GOD stands forever."
(ISAIAH 40:8)**

sight of GOD and that they may have everlasting life with HIM in heaven when HE returns.

The death and resurrection of CHRIST was part of GOD'S SOVEREIGN WILL for the salvation of entire humankind that chose to believe in HIM before the foundations of the world as mentioned in the book of Ephesians chapter 1. This gift of salvation that GOD has given by grace alone and through faith alone in JESUS CHRIST is the true spiritual blessing which all true Christians are talking about. No other religion in the history that their leader died to save them from eternal condemnation. This is the reason Christians talk about JESUS CHRIST THE NAME THAT IS ABOVE EVERY OTHER NAME.

The hall mark of Christianity is the love that is proved among believers. Love is the center for Christianity. It is important to always devote yourself to the Christian lifestyle including being holy. Yes, the Christian path is not an easy one, but Christ promised that He will always be with us. Life can be very hard and annoying indeed. There is so much concern happening in the world currently. As believers we seek refuge and unshakeable faith in God who is our permanent hiding place. This topic is of profound significance. The subject is everyday religiousness. It put forward a question which stresses the attention of all confessing Christians-Are we holy? Shall we see the Lord? Holiness is an all-time practice. I mean holiness is not a seasonal event. The Bible made it clear that "There is a time to weep, and a time to laugh-a time to keep silence, and a time to speak" (Eccles. 3:4, 7); but there is no time, no, not a moment, in which Christians ought not to be holy. True or false? We must always be holy unto GOD.

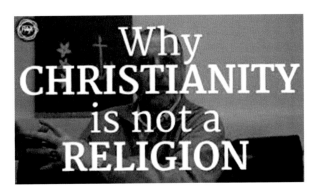

In Hebrews (12:14 KJV), we were instructed to follow peace with all men, and holiness, without which no man shall see the LORD. The question is having GOD lowered His standard? No let every man be lairs and God alone be truthful. "Without holiness, no man shall see the Lord" (Hebrews 12:14). I shall try, by God's help, to examine what true holiness is, and the reason it is so needful.

"The grass withers and the flowers fade,
But the word of our GOD stands forever."
(ISAIAH 40:8)

What does it mean to pursue holiness? It is an easy thing in today's world to pursue after holiness. What will be our benefits as Christians to pursue holiness? The Scripture made it clear that without holiness no one can see GOD.

If we want to spend eternity with the LORD JESUS, we must do everything in our power to attain holiness. God is not respecter of any person. We cannot expect to spend eternity with HIM when we do not leave a holy life. "If we say that we have fellowship with him, and walk in darkness, we lie, and do not the truth: 7 But if we walk in the light, as he is in the light, we have fellowship one with another, and the blood of Jesus Christ his Son cleanseth us from all sin. 8 If we say that we have no sin, we deceive ourselves, and the truth is not in us." (1st John 1:6-8).

- Holiness is the practice of being of one mind with GOD, according as we find HIS mind defined in Scripture. It is the habit of harmonizing in GOD'S judgement-hating what HE hates-loving what HE loves-and measuring everything in this world by the standard of HIS Word. A man or woman who totally agrees with GOD, he/she is the most holy man/woman.

- A holy man/woman will try to avoid every known sin and to keep every known commandment. He/she will have an absolute set of minds to GOD, an enthusiastic desire to do HIS will-a greater fear of displeasing Him than of displeasing the world, and love to all HIS ways. He will feel what Paul felt when he said, "I delight in the law of God after the inward man" (Romans 7:22), and what David felt when he said, "I esteem all Thy precepts concerning all things to be right, and I hate every false way" (Psalms 119:128).

- Any man or woman in pursuit of holiness will always strive to be like our Lord JESUS CHRIST. A believer will not only live the life of faith in HIM and draw from HIM all his/her daily peace and strength but will also labor to have the mind that was in HIM and to be "conformed to HIS image" (Romans 8:29). Christian desires to bear with and forgive others, even as Christ forgave us-to be unselfish, even as Christ pleased not HIMSELF-to walk in love, even as Christ loved us-to be lowly-minded and humble, even as CHRIST made HIMSELF of no reputation and humbled HIMSELF. Pursuit of holiness requires us believers to follow abstinence and self-denial. He/she will make every effort to mortify the desires of his/her body-to crucify the flesh with his/her affections and lusts-to curb one is passions-to restrain himself/herself carnal feelings, lest at any time they break loose. The LORD JESUS said to HIS Apostles, "Take heed to yourselves, lest at any time your hearts be overcharged with surfeiting and drunkenness, and cares of this life" (Luke 21:34); and that of the Apostle Paul, "I keep under my body, and bring it into subjection, lest that by any means when I have preached to others, I myself should be a castaway" (1 Corinthians 9:27).

**"The grass withers and the flowers fade,
But the word of our GOD stands forever."
(ISAIAH 40:8)**

- The pursuit of holiness demands one to follow meekness, long-suffering, gentleness, patience, kind tempers, and the control of his/her tongue.

The man or woman will bear much, forbear much, overlook much, and be slow to talk of standing on his/her rights. A Classical example of this in the behavior of King David when Shimei cursed him-and Moses, a man who saw GOD face-face when Aaron and Miriam his siblings spoke against him (2 Samuel 16:10; Numbers 12:3). Pursuing holiness requires self-denial. One who is after holiness fears the LORD with all his or her mind? Will not compromise with any form of unrighteousness. Will stand firm and stand tall for God like Daniel, Nehemiah, Hezekiah, Shedrach, Meshack and Abednego, Esther, and Mordechai. We must be holy because this is the only proof that we love the Lord Jesus Christ in honesty. This is a point on which HE has spoken most plainly, in the fourteenth and fifteenth chapters of John. "If ye love Me, keep my commandments." "He that hath my commandments and keepeth them, he it is that loveth Me."- "If a man loves Me, he will keep my words."- "Ye are my friends if ye do whatsoever I command you" (John 14:15, 21, 23; 15:14).

We cannot be holy without abiding in CHRIST. JESUS says HIMSELF, "Abide in ME and I in you, he that abideth in ME and I in him, the same beareth much fruit" (John 15:4, 5). It pleased the Father that in Him should all fullness dwell-a full supply for all a believer's wants. He is the healer of all healers (the greatest Physician) to whom you must daily go, if you would continue to enjoy good health. He is the Holy Manna which you must eat daily, and the fountain of living water which you must drink daily. His arm is the arm on which you must lean daily, as you come up out of the desert of this world. You must not only be rooted, but you must also lean on Him.

The Apostle Paul was a man that fears GOD with all his heart, his mind, indeed-a holy man-a rising, thriving Christian-and what was the secret of it all? He was one to whom CHRIST was "all in all." He was ever "looking unto Jesus." He wrote "I can do all things," "through Christ which strengthens me." "I live, yet not I, but Christ liveth in me. The life that I now live, I live by the faith of the Son of God." Let us do likewise (Hebrews 12:2; Philippians 4:13; Galatians 2:20). Beloved as you read this book, know these things by experience, and not by unfounded information only. May the Holy Spirit of God give us clear vision of the importance

"The grass withers and the flowers fade,
But the word of our GOD stands forever."
(ISAIAH 40:8)

of holiness, far more than we can ever imagine in Jesus' name Amen. I earnestly pray that our years be holy years with our souls, and then they will be happy ones. Whether we live, may we live unto the Lord; or whether we die, May we die unto the Lord; or if Jesus Christ comes for us, may we be found in peace, without spot, and righteous!

Friends, cleaving unto the LORD will help us to be holy until the end of our Christian race. "Be you therefore very courageous to keep and to do all that is written in the book of the Law of Moses" (Joshua 23:6-13). This will involve individual devotion: God seeks the devotion of our hearts. It is internal and spiritual, and not simply a fact of noticeable behavior.

**"The grass withers and the flowers fade,
But the word of our GOD stands forever."
(ISAIAH 40:8)**

It suggests drawing near to God in prayer, walking with God, delighting in Him, looking to be like Him, aiming at pleasing Him. The word of the must be obeyed to the core. Joshua exhorts the people to "be very courageous," "to keep and to do all that is written in the book of the law of Moses." Devotion of heart is a mockery unless it leads to obedience in conduct. We must cleave to God in action as well as in feeling. Joshua encouraged purity. The people are exhorted to avoid the contamination of heathen society and the sin of idolatry. Anything that takes the place of God in our heart is an idol. All sinful pleasures and worldly interests that are not consistent with pure devotion to God separate us from Him and vitiate our service. God cannot accept our sacrifices while we approach Him with sinful affections (Isaiah 1:18).

The holy Bible instructed us to be holy because the voice of God in Scripture simply commands it. The Lord Jesus says to His people, "Except your righteousness shall exceed the righteousness of the scribes and Pharisees, ye shall in no case enter into the kingdom of heaven" (Matthew 5:20). "Be ye perfect, even as your Father which is in heaven is perfect" (Matthew 5:48). Paul tells the Thessalonians, "This is the will of God, even your sanctification" (1 Thessalonians. 4:3). And Peter says, "As He which hath called you is holy, so be ye holy in all manner of conversation; because it is written, 'Be ye holy, for I am holy'" (1 Peter 1:15, 16).

In conclusion, we must be holy, because without holiness on earth we shall never step into heaven to see our HOLY FATHER and our LORD and SAVIOR JESUS CHRIST. Heaven is prepared for holy people. Heaven is a holy place. The LORD of heaven is a HOLY BEING. Angels are holy creatures. Holiness is written on everything in heaven. The book of Revelation says specifically, "There shall in no wise enter into it anything that defileth, neither whatsoever worketh abomination, or maketh a lie" (Revelations 21:27). My dear brothers and sisters in CHRIST are appealing to everyone who reads this book, the fact is that we cannot Death waits for no one. Death or rapture can occur any moment. No time to waste. The grave makes no

"The grass withers and the flowers fade, But the word of our GOD stands forever." (ISAIAH 40:8)

modification. Each will rise again with the same character in which he breathed his last. Where will you spend your last breath now? There is no repentance in heaven or inside the grave. Now is the time for each one of us to make it right. Where will our place be if we are foreigners to holiness now? "To be conformed to the image of God's Son" is the summary of the total matter. "To as many as receive Him, He gives power to become sons of God" (Acts 5:31; John 1:12, 13). The fact is that Holiness comes from CHRIST. It is the result of a dynamic union with HIM. It comes only when you have continuous close relationship with GOD. It is only when we keep a covenant relationship with CHRIST JESUS who saved us from the hand Satan. It is the fruit of being a living branch of our LORD and SAVIOR JESUS CHRIST who is the **TRUE VINE**. You can pray to GOD to help you to be holy and to teach you to do HIS will.

"The grass withers and the flowers fade, But the word of our GOD stands forever." (ISAIAH 40:8)

CHAPTER 5

CHRIST WILL RETURN

Prophecies About Messiah:

It is important to clarify important issues or event preceding CHRIST return. But let me go back when GOD promised to send the MESSIAH to be born from the tribe of David who will eventually save the entire humanity from their wickedness. JESUS was born in Bethlehem of Judaea. Our GOD is covenant keeper. GOD is a promise-keeper. A well-known fact is that JESUS was of Jewish origin and therefore was the seed of Abraham. We are told that through Abraham's offspring "all nations on earth will be blessed." We Christians believe that the fulfillment of this divine promise is JESUS CHRIST (Genesis 22:18). We also know that JESUS is from the lineage of Jacob, Abraham's grandson "I see him, but not now; I behold him, but not nearby. A star will come out of Jacob; a scepter will rise out of Israel." (Numbers 24:17).

He is from the line of Jesse, the father of King David: "A shoot will come up from the stump of Jesse; from his roots a branch will bear fruit. The spirit of the Lord will rest on him." (Isaiah 11:1). Christ is from the line of King David: "The days are coming, declares the Lord, when I will raise up for David a righteous Branch, a King who will reign wisely and do what is just and right in the land. This is the name by which he will be called: the Lord our righteous savior." (Jeremiah 23:5-6). "Rejoice, O daughter of Zion! Shout aloud, O daughter of Jerusalem! Behold, your king is coming to you; righteous and having salvation is He, humble and mounted on a donkey, on a colt, the foal of a donkey" (Zechariah 9:9).

"The grass withers and the flowers fade,
But the word of our GOD stands forever."
(ISAIAH 40:8)

The Four Prophecies that Matthew Quotes

1. Jesus' virgin brith (Isaiah 7:4)

2. Bethlehem as the location of Jesus' birth (Micah 5:2)

3. Jospeh, Mary and Jesus travel to Egypt (Hosea 11:1)

4. The Slaughter of the innocents (Jeremiah 31:15)

Why does Matthew quote these four prophecies?

Hail Mary

Hail Mary, full of grace,
the Lord is with thee.
Blessed art thou among
women, and blessed is
the fruit of thy womb Jesus.
Holy Mary, Mother of God,
pray for us sinners,
now and at the hour
of our death.
Amen.

"The grass withers and the flowers fade,
But the word of our GOD stands forever."
(ISAIAH 40:8)

Mary's Divine Encounter With Angel Gabriel!

And in the sixth month the angel Gabriel was sent from God unto a city of Galilee, named Nazareth, To a virgin espoused to a man whose name was Joseph, of the house of David; and the virgin's name was Mary. And the angel came in unto her, and said, Hail, thou that art highly favoured, the Lord is with thee: blessed art thou among women.

And when she saw him, she was troubled at what he was saying and cast in her mind what manner of salutation this should be. And the angel said unto her, Fear not, Mary: for thou hast found favors with God. And behold, thou shalt conceive in thy womb, and bring forth a son, and shalt call his name JESUS. He shall be great and shall be called the Son of the Highest: and the Lord God shall give unto him the throne of his father David: And he shall reign over the house of Jacob for ever; and of his kingdom there shall be no end. Then said Mary unto the angel, How shall this be, seeing I know not a man? And the angel answered and said unto her, The Holy Ghost shall come upon thee, and the power of the Highest shall overshadow thee: therefore also that holy thing which shall be born of thee shall be called the Son of God" (Luke 1:26-35).

**"The grass withers and the flowers fade,
But the word of our GOD stands forever."
(ISAIAH 40:8)**

The virgin birth was first mention in Genesis 3:15, which the Scripture promised that "the seed of woman" would be the victor over Satan and sin. It was specifically predicted in the book of Isaiah 7:14: "Behold, a virgin will be with child and bear a son, and she will call His name Immanuel" (Isaiah 7:14). "For unto us a child is born, unto us a son is given: and the government shall be upon his shoulder: and his name shall be called Wonderful, Counsellor, The mighty God, The everlasting Father, The Prince of Peace. Of the increase of his government and peace there shall be no end, upon the throne of David, and upon his kingdom, to order it, and to set it up with judgment and with justice from henceforth even for ever. The zeal of the Lord of hosts will perform this" (Isaiah 9:6-7). This prophecy came to fulfillment in the Book of Matthew 1:22-23, in Virgin Mary. She is called a "virgin" in Luke 1:27. Mary did not conceive through ordinary means, but through the Holy Spirit.

- JESUS IS THE SON OF GOD

- HE IS SINLESS; HE NEW NO SIN

- HE WAS NOT CONCEIVED IN SIN

- EVERY ONE OF US WAS CONCEIVED IN SIN.

- BUT NOT JESUS CHRIST, THE SON OF THE HIGHEST GOD ALMIGHTY.

This was God's astounding intervention, creating descendants without a human father. No man or angel was involved. CHRIST, who was GOD from all eternity, took hold of this human nature thus conceived and joined it to HIMSELF.

What is the birth of the virgin? The essential need originated in humans. Every normal, human birth produces another sinner, just as Adam, as sinner, produced a race of sinners. Our Savior had to be genuinely human and truthfully sinless to be our faultless substitute and pay our consequence of guilt before an infinite GOD by HIS death. Without the virgin birth, there would be no salvation for sinners. JESUS CHRIST would be a sinful human being. If the virgin birth did not occur, then the Bible is not true and cannot be trusted. In short, it is an essential part of salvation and of Scripture. Through Adam death came to human race. But JESUS CHRIST life eternal was restored to those who will make room for CHRIST and accept HIS agony on the cross more than 2,000 years back.

The Bible made it clear that we should always be vigilant so the coming of LORD JESUS will not take us unaware. Nonetheless it also teaches that no one can say for certain that we are living in the "end times." This is at best a debatable proposition. JESUS Himself recurrently said that no one knows the day or hour of CHRIST return (Matthew 24:36; Mark 13:32; Acts 1:7). Without a doubt, we are surrounded by events and developments that could be interpreted as signs of the end of time. On every hand we see famines, earthquakes, disasters, troubles, persecutions, wars, and rumors of wars (Mark 13:7-9).

**"The grass withers and the flowers fade,
But the word of our GOD stands forever."
(ISAIAH 40:8)**

But then again has there ever been a period in the history of the world when this was not the case? When the disciples came to Jesus and asked Him, 'what will be the sign of your coming, and of the end of the age?' He told them things were going to get worse before they got better. Then He added these words: see to it that you are not alarmed...' (Matthew 24:6 NIV) The word alarmed is one JESUS used only on this occasion; it means 'to wail, to cry aloud.' In actual sense, what the LORD was saying is this: 'Don't fall apart when bad things happen.'

Let us look at some of the sign's JESUS said would herald HIS return. Spiritual deception. 'Watch out that no one deceives you. For many will come in My name, claiming, "I am the Messiah," and will deceive many.' (Matthew 24:4–5 NIV) Take note that there will be many deceivers in the world and as a result many will be deceived. JESUS also said they will come 'in My name,' masquerading as ministers of God and claiming special position and higher spirituality. They will boast of insider evidence and adorn their knowledges with phrases like 'God told me,' inferring they have access to information the common people like us do not have. Do not be deceived. JESUS also warned, '...false Messiahs and false prophets will appear and perform great signs and wonders to deceive, if possible, even the elect.' (Matthew 24:24 NIV) Multitudes and miracles—when you see them, are careful. Satan can counterfeit both. Be spiritually diligent. Focus on one question: 'Is this person pointing listeners to the real, Biblical JESUS?' There is only room for one name on the tent—and that's JESUS!

Jesus said: 'You hear of wars and rumours of wars see to it that you are not alarmed. Such things must happen, but the end is still to come. Nations will rise against nation, and kingdom against kingdom. There will be famines and earthquakes in various places. All these are the beginning of birth pains.' Jesus said, 'All these are the beginning of birth pains.' Rejoice! GOD is still on the throne. HIS plan is still being worked out. The death throes of the old order we live in are the 'birth pains' of a new and glorious order, when Christ will return to set up HIS Kingdom. Jesus said to His disciples: you will be handed over to be persecute put to death, and hated by all nations because of Me. At that time many will turn away from the faith and will betray and hate each other, and many false prophets will appear and deceive many people. Because of the increase of wickedness, the love of most will grow cold.' (Matthew 24:9–12 NIV). Take notice the words 'put to death.' There is no doubt that those who have already fulfilled this prophecy are in Heaven. Unbelievably hatred of Christians is more today than ever. According to Voice of the Martyrs, a Christian agency that protects religious liberties contends that more of CHRIST'S followers have been killed for their faith in the last period than in most of the previous centuries put together.

The global evangelism movement "reports an average of 165,000 martyrs a year, more than four times the number in the past century". According to statics, currently countries that ease religious freedom are experiencing increasing hostility toward Christians e.g., United States of America. Respected Professors in a Higher Institution publicly mock Bible-believing students today. TV talk show hosts make mockery of people of faith. We can expect the persecution to increase, and when it does, fragile beliefs will collapse and 'the love of many will grow cold' (Matthew 24:12 NLT).

> **"The grass withers and the flowers fade,**
> **But the word of our GOD stands forever."**
> **(ISAIAH 40:8)**

Jesus said when we see calamity and apostasy, do not give in to fear because they are signs of HIS imminent return. 'But he who endures to the end shall be saved. And this Gospel of the Kingdom will be preached in the entire world as a witness to all the nations, and then the end will come.' (Matthew 24:13–14 NKJV) Every prophecy concerning Christ's first coming was fulfilled in detail, and so will every prophecy concern HIS second coming. Our mandate is to work, pray, give, and take the Gospel to the whole world until then will CHRIST return. The truth is that the church is going down like Gideon's army, and the world is in a state of turmoil, do not react excessively. 'Be still in the presence of the Lord and wait patiently for HIM to act. He says, "Be still, and know that I am God; I will be exalted among the nations, I will be exalted in the earth." (Psalm 46:10 NIV). Do not worry all we need to do is to put our trust in ALL and MIGHTY GOD.

With JESUS on our side, we will make it to the end by HIS SPECIAL grace. "For the Lord himself will come down from heaven, with a loud command, with the voice of the archangel and with the trumpet call of God, and the dead in Christ will rise first. After that, we who are still alive and are left will be caught up together with them in the clouds to meet the Lord in the air. And so, we will be with the Lord forever" (1Thessalonians 4:16-17 NIV). And the Bible says that we should be ready CHRIST can come back any time. He says that HE will come when we do not expect. HE is coming like a thief at night. Are you ready? Please be ready no more to waste. CHRIST can appear any moment from now.

In conclusion, CHRIST will surely return as HE promised.

"The grass withers and the flowers fade,
But the word of our GOD stands forever."
(ISAIAH 40:8)

CHAPTER 6

SIGNS OF CHRIST'S RETURN!

What will the world be like just before CHRIST returns?

As In The Days Of Noah

The world just before CHRIST'S return will be filled with LAWLESSNESS that is shown, as if to insult GOD. We have in every way challenged GOD'S own AUTHORITY. Add to that the stressed relationships between the political groups and religious groups everywhere in the world, and we are indeed at the edge of blowing up the entire world. CHRIST'S return to the earth is unquestionably needed for one reason: human survival/continued existence. Lawlessness has become a World Problems & Global Issues.

Lawlessness is a lack of law, in any of the numerous right minds of that word. Lawlessness may describe various conditions. Lawlessness is a behavior that is illegal or not controlled by laws: Our lovely country U.S.A. has fall away into lawlessness. For example, there seems to be an increasing sense of lawlessness in our border regions. People are terrified of murder, theft, assaults, and general lawlessness. "And because lawlessness shall abound, the love of many shall wax cold. 13 But he that shall endure unto the end, the same shall be saved (Mat 24:12-13).

The Gospel according to Matthew mentioned specific events which will happen before the return of CHRIST. The sign of end time events is all over the place. It is only those individuals who do not have a personal relationship with JESUS CHRIST will be completely unaware of these signs of HIS return. I am personally convinced than ever that the return of CHRIST is at hand. The word of GOD made it clear of all the signs that will go ahead before the return of JESUS CHRIST. For us to know all these signs will help us to understand the events and to redeem the time. These day and age we use the navigators to know and follow directions. I am not good at directions. Knowing the right directions keeps me away from the danger of going the wrong way. Christians do believe GOD is in control of all things and has a plan for the end of the world.

- **The end of this world will come:** JESUS spoke about the end of the world. HE explained how the earth will one day pass away. HE also shared that there will be an increase in earthquakes, famines, wars, and pandemics before the end. But, in the book of Revelation, the apostle John shared how GOD will then create a new heaven and new earth.

- **Just how it will happen is mysterious:** JESUS was very clear that no one knows when the end will come. HE explained that he would one day return at a time that no one expected, like a thief in the night. Followers of JESUS are therefore encouraged to "be ready."

> "The grass withers and the flowers fade,
> But the word of our GOD stands forever."
> (ISAIAH 40:8)

- **JESUS promises aid to face every single challenge of life:** Believers were never promised to have trouble free life than other people. However, JESUS does promise to help those who ask through any and every trouble of life. Nothing you will ever face in your life can surprise GOD, not even the end of the world.

"FOR THE LORD HIMSELF SHALL DESCEND FROM HEAVEN, WITH A SHOUT."

1 Thessalonians 4:16

The signs of Christ's return

Today we are talking about signs of the times. God has given us signs in his word that he is returning and even as it gets near, he is giving us specific signs to let us know that his return is very near. Signs are extremely helpful. Signs help you get on the right highway or go in the right direction. The right street signs help us. I mean, when I am on the highway, I am looking for signs for the food. Signs also give us warnings. Signs keep us from danger. Aren't you glad for the signs that keep you from danger? Give you warnings. JESUS in HIS infinite mercy gave us a detailed sign like this. Apostle Paul's words right after he wrote about the rapture in

Thessalonians: "1 But concerning the times and the seasons, brethren, you have no need that I should write to you. 2 For you know perfectly that the day of the Lord so comes as a thief in the night. 3 For when they say, "Peace and safety!" then sudden destruction comes upon them, as labor pains upon a pregnant woman. And they shall not escape" (1st Thessalonians 5:1-3).

Paul continues this in Thessalonians 5:4-6, "But you, brothers, and sisters, are not in darkness so that this day should surprise you like a thief. You are all children of the light and children of the day. We do not belong to the night or to the darkness. So then, let us not be like others who are asleep but let us be awake and sober." Currently, I want to mention some signs that signify the return of JESUS CHRIST is near than what we think.

These are some of the signs of HIS return:
Deceptive Spirit: False CHRISTS saying, "I am the MESSIAH"
Matthew 24:3-14

"The grass withers and the flowers fade,
But the word of our GOD stands forever."
(ISAIAH 40:8)

It is important to be GRANDED IN THE WORD OF GOD: Let us first walk through the first few verses in Matthew 24:3-5 and the incredible passage say:

As JESUS was sitting on the Mount of Olives, the disciples came to HIM privately. 3 "Tell us," they said, "when will this happen and what will be the sign of your coming and of the end of the age?" 4 Jesus answered: "Watch out that no one deceives you. 5 For many will come in my name, claiming, 'I am the MESSIAH,' and will deceive many." JESUS says false Christs deceiving people will be a sign. Do not forget that JESUS said false Christ that will come, saying, "I am the Messiah." That is a big sign that the coming of the LORD is very nearby.

Wars And Rumors Of Wars: Kingdom Against Kingdom

- We will hear wars and rumors of wars, or you will hear about global and political unrest. Those are signs in Matthew 24:6-8, "You will hear of wars and rumors of wars but see to it that you are not alarmed. Such things must happen, but the end is still to come. 7 Nation will rise against nation and kingdom against kingdom. There will be famines and earthquakes in various places." 8 All these are the beginning of sorrows.

Severe Persecution Against CHRIST Followers From

All Nations For HIS Sake:

- Friends, this is already happening around the world. Over twenty thousand Christians have been tortured and murdered in Nigerian because of their belief in the LORD CHRIST. Our LORD JESUS said this in Matthew 24:8, "All these are the beginning of sorrows." All of these are the beginning of the coming of the LORD. When you see these things, these signs, it is near. Matthew 24:9, "Then you will be handed over to be persecuted and put to death and you will be hated by all nations because of me." JESUS here is speaking of increased pressure and persecution against CHRIST followers. We are aware of that around the world. According to the latest world watch list from open doors, around 215 million Christians face significant levels of persecution in the world today. According to Researchers, shows that one in 12 Christians live where their faith is illegal, not allowed, or punished. JESUS said this kind of persecution is a sign that HE will return. Christian are being slaughtered like chicken every day.

"The grass withers and the flowers fade,
But the word of our GOD stands forever."
(ISAIAH 40:8)

Betrayal Of One Another And Shall Hating One Another

- Matthew 24:10-11, "At that time, many will turn away from the faith and will betray and hate each other, and many false prophets will appear and deceive many people." There will be great deception before the coming of the Lord. We do not want to be deceived these days.

False Prophets Shall Rise; The Gospel Shall Be Preached Everywhere In The World

- Matthew 24:12-14 says, "because of the increase of wickedness, the love of most will grow cold, 13 but the one who stands firm to the end will be saved. 14 And this gospel of the kingdom will be preached to the whole world as a testimony to all nations and then the end will come." An impressive sign of the return of CHRIST is that the gospel of JESUS CHRIST is going to be preached to all nations. It is going to be preached around the world. There is going to be an intensifying of global mission efforts around the world to get the gospel out to every person.

Perilous Time Shall Come:

The Bible made it clear that in the last days, perilous times will come. Are we now living in perilous times? We have all seen the deadly disease called (Corvid 19) that terrorized the entire universe. More than 5 million people lost their lives. In addition, we see nation invading another nation, we have rumors of wars, other diseases, strong storms, earthquakes, (over 43 million people died in Syria and Türkiye just less than 2 months ago, and there is civil unrest in most countries including United State of America etc.

- "You should know this Timothy said that in the last days there will be very difficult times. 2 For people will love only themselves and their money. They will be boastful and proud, scoffing at God, disobedient to their parents, and ungrateful. They will consider nothing sacred. 3They will be unloving and unforgiving; they will slander others and have no self-control. They will be cruel and hate what is good. 4They will betray their friends, be reckless, be puffed up with pride, and love pleasure rather than God. 5They will act religious, but they will reject the power that could make them godly. Stay away from people like that! 6They are the kind who work their way into people's homes and win the confidence of vulnerable women who are burdened with the guilt of sin and

**"The grass withers and the flowers fade,
But the word of our GOD stands forever."
(ISAIAH 40:8)**

controlled by various desires.7(Such women are forever following new teachings, but they are never able to understand the truth.) 8 These teachers oppose the truth just as Jannes and Jambres opposed Moses. They have depraved minds and a counterfeit faith. 9 But they will not get away with this for long. Someday everyone will recognize what fools they are, just as with Jannes and Jambres" 2nd Timothy 3:1-9).

**"The grass withers and the flowers fade,
But the word of our GOD stands forever."
(ISAIAH 40:8)**

CHAPTER 7

DO NOT DROP YOUR CROWNS

How is it that after claiming that we are heading to heaven and yet we miss our crowns? Is this possible? Yes, it is possible that we miss our crown. We are all in a race. We are expected to run to the end and lay our crown at the feet of JESUS CHRIST. Let us look at the earthly sports activities: those who are engaged in marathons, not all of them will get a prize. It is only when you run to the end that you get a prize. Even in our pursuit of education, if we do not go through with our curriculum and finish every subject that is required, we are able to graduate and obtain our certificate. Friends the only way for us not to miss our crown is to continue to serve God in the spirit and in truth. If we become careless in our Christian race, we will miss our crown. Sin will be the grass root of what will make us miss our crown in Heaven.

Like I mentioned earlier on, Heaven is a prepared place for prepared people. When Apostle Paul was writing to the Christians in the book of Hebrew, he encouraged us to run the race with perseverance. In Hebrews 12:1-3 "Therefore, since we are surrounded by such a huge crowd of witnesses to the life of faith, let us strip off every weight that slows us down, especially the sin that so easily trips us up. And let us run with endurance the race God has set before us." We do this by keeping our eyes on Jesus, the champion who starts and perfects our faith. Because of the joy awaiting HIM, HE endured the cross, ignoring its shame. Now HE is seated in the place of honor beside GOD'S throne. Think of all the antagonism he endured from sinful people; then you will not become weary and give up" (NLT). This was written by Apostle Paul to encourage and challenge believers to persevere in our faith, particularly during all that is happening under our watch today in the world.

Determination not to miss our crown depends on our decision now. Tell yourself I will run to win the race that is set before me. Our goal as believers is to spend time without end with JESUS CHRIST OUR LORD AND SAVIOUR. We need to tell ourselves that we are not candidates for hell fire in JESUS name Amen. If any one of us goes to hell it will be terrible after the agony and humiliation that our LORD went through for us on the Cross of Calvary. 2nd Corinthians 5:10 "For we must all appear before the judgment seat of Christ, so that each one may be paid back according to what he has done while in the body, whether good or evil" (KJV). So, friends, how we live here right now matters if we will qualify for the crown if at all that we made it to Heaven. We must make to obtain all the mentioned below crowns if we continue do the will and work faithfully for GOD and HIS CHRIST.

> **"The grass withers and the flowers fade,**
> **But the word of our GOD stands forever."**
> **(ISAIAH 40:8)**

There Are Different Crowns:

The Bible communicated to us of five defined crowns we can obtain in heaven. You will notice they tend to overlap.

The Crown of Glory- given to those who long for Jesus' reappearance. HIS glory refers to HIS nature, the praise and honor HE deserves, and the blessing of finally being in His presence.

1st Peter 5:4 "And when the Chief Shepherd appears, you will receive the crown of glory that does not fade away" (KJV).

Crown of Righteousness- given to us through Jesus' righteousness only. HE shares it with only those who faithfully serve HIM and others, and who long to see HIM.

"Finally, there is laid up for me the crown of righteousness, which the LORD, the RIGHTEOUS JUDGE, will give to me on that day, and not only to me but also to all who have loved HIS appearing" (2nd Timothy 4:8).

Crown of Rejoicing- given to those who long to be in JESUS'S presence and are always thankful for HIS blessings. This crown includes GOD'S promise of no tears, sorrow, death, crying, or pain in heaven (Revelation 21:4).

"For what is our hope, or joy, or crown of rejoicing? Is it not even you in the presence of our Lord Jesus Christ at His coming?" (1st Thessalonians 2:19).

The Imperishable Crown- Is a special crown given to those who endured through every circumstance and remained faithful to the LORD. Because the LORD is everlasting, so is the crown we receive if we finish our race well.

"Do you not know that those who run in a race all run, but one receives the prize? Run in such a way that you may obtain it. And everyone who competes for the prize is temperate disciplined in all things. Now they do it to obtain a perishable crown, but we do it for an imperishable crown" (1st Corinthians 9:24-25).

The Crown of Life- for all believers who withstood suffering and bravely defended their faith. It does not refer to the gift of eternal life which comes through JESUS CHRIST alone.

"Do not fear any of those things which you are about to suffer. Indeed, the devil is about to throw some of you into prison, that you may be tested, and you will have tribulation ten days. Be faithful until death, and I will give you the crown of life" (Revelation 2:10). My brothers and sisters in the LORD, it will not be to our benefit if we should lose the above-mentioned crowns after our hard work for the LORD here on earth.

> **"The grass withers and the flowers fade,
> But the word of our GOD stands forever."
> (ISAIAH 40:8)**

CHAPTER 8

RUN TO THE END

Alongside crowns, we will receive other rewards when we stand before the Lord one day. The Bible presents these as promises from God for those who endure to the end. Christian race is not a day journey but a journey that will endure throughout your life. You must be strong, stand tall, stand still, determine in your heart that come what I may run to the of this race I am engaged in. In this generation, we are currently in a state where everything goes. Nothing is wrong anymore. There is so much division among so-called Christians. We are mandated to "hold fast" and to stand firm in Jesus. Staying strong in CHRIST is the key to the whole issue. If you are abiding in JESUS CHRIST, then you are obeying. Are you abiding in God? Are you reading the Word and praying regularly? Are you surrendering to Him daily? Are you leaning on His power and infinite resources to help you overcome sin and temptation? Are you allowing Him to work through you and in you? Are you sharing His blessings with others?

Abide in the Lord. Hold fast to Him. Keep fighting the good fight and finish your race well. Remember that walking in faith is not a sprint, it is a marathon. So, hang in there until you cross the finish line, and the Lord says to you, "Well done, good and faithful servant." In our Christian life, we run the race of faith. We do not struggle for the crown that only one can obtain. We try to finish strong in our faith. When we cross the finishing line the GOD makes us all victors. Just like the athletic runners, we must lay aside interferences of our endurance. Therefore, since we are surrounded by so great a cloud of witnesses, let us also lay aside every weight, and sin which clings so closely, and let us run with endurance the race that is set before us, looking to Jesus, the founder and perfecter of our faith, who for the joy that was set before him endured the cross, despising the shame, and is seated at the right hand of the throne of God.

Consider HIM who endured from sinners such hostility towards himself, so that you may not grow weary or fainthearted. Also, as believers, we work hard to fortify our faith to endure the race of our faith. We must seek HIM daily in HIS word and in prayer. We must seek constant fellowship among other believers and let our fellow Church members encourage us in the faith. It is necessary for us as the body of CHRIST welcome rebuke and embrace trials. If we are to keep our eyes focused on JESUS CHRIST our SAVIOR, personal discipline becomes essential. What is our benefit if we do not run this race to the end? Christian's goals are to run and spend eternity with CHRIST. JESUS promised us that HE is going to prepare a place in Heaven for us and after HE prepare the place, HE will come back to take us home to HIMSELF. Paul writes to the Corinthian Church about the Christian life. "Know ye not that they which run in a race run all, but one receiveth the prize? So run, that ye may obtain" (1st Corinthians 924).

> **"The grass withers and the flowers fade,**
> **But the word of our GOD stands forever."**
> **(ISAIAH 40:8)**

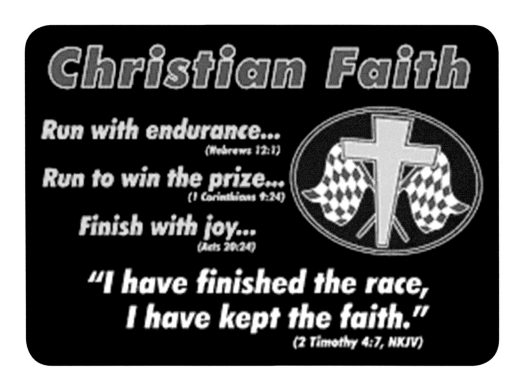

Christian Faith

Run with endurance...
(Hebrews 12:1)

Run to win the prize...
(1 Corinthians 9:24)

Finish with joy...
(Acts 20:24)

"I have finished the race,
I have kept the faith."
(2 Timothy 4:7, NKJV)

The Corinthians thought they could live as they pleased now; they were saved. They believed their spiritual freedom gave them rights and privileges others did not have. They coined phrases, like, "all things are lawful for me, "and " food is for the body and the body is for food. "So, Paul responded to these beliefs by saying this in 1 Corinthians 6:12-13: All things are lawful for me, but all things are not helpful. All things are lawful for me, but I will not be brought under the power of any. Foods for the stomach and the stomach for foods, but God will destroy both it and them. Now the body is not for sexual immorality but for the Lord, and the Lord for the body. Paul continues to challenge the Corinthians about their liberty until the end of chapter 11.

In chapter 9 Paul defends the right of those who preach the gospel to be supported by the Church. But he did not use this right, so that he could preach the gospel freely and not have it identified with the charlatans and philosophers of his day. Paul was willing to forget his rights for the benefit of others and he said the Corinthians should do the same. They should not place an obstacle before unbelievers and weaker brothers by living for themselves. At the end of chapter 9, Paul uses the analogy of running a race to describe the Christian life. It is like running a marathon, a long-distance race that requires preparation and endurance. "Therefore we also, since we are surrounded by so great a cloud of witnesses, let us lay aside every weight, and the sin which so easily ensnares us, and let us run with endurance the race that is set before us" (Hebrew 12:1).

"The grass withers and the flowers fade,
But the word of our GOD stands forever."
(ISAIAH 40:8)

47

The writer to the Hebrews says we are to lay aside every weight and the sin that so easily ensnares us. A weight is not the same thing as a sin. A weight does not break God's law, but it does hinder us in the Christian race. Weight is something that sidetracks us from more significant things. A sports man or woman wanting to win in a particular race will get rid of weight so that they can concentrate on running the race to win.

Do Not Give Up!

Keep Running Your Race of Faith Without Looking Back

With all my personal experiences in this Christian race, there has been a time when I am feeling like I can never continue because of circumstances beyond my control. There have been challenges one after the other. The first of them all is health issues. But in all these, my GOD has been faithful and merciful. What do you do when the doctor tells you that there is no medical intervention with your health situation? At one point, I must leave my job due to my inability to function due to health challenge. As a Registered Nurse I must lift at least 10 pounds, but I could not even lift 5 pounds. Not to talk about to eat or take my medication unless my husband comes back from work, or a Christian sister comes to lend a helping hand. It is a blessing to be in good health.

Inspite of all these challenges, I am determined to run this race that is set before me until I meet my JESUS. JESUS did not promise us that following HIM will be easy. But with JESUS in the vessel, we shall always smile at the storm of life. As believers, we cannot avoid trials and temptations. JESUS HIMSELVE went through the worst. All the Apostles of JESUS CHRIST were all murdered in a humiliating way. All we need is the strength to continue with perseverance and patience.

"The grass withers and the flowers fade,
But the word of our GOD stands forever."
(ISAIAH 40:8)

My encouragement came from the Book of Matthew 24:13. "But he that shall endure unto the end, the same shall be saved." (Matthew 24:13). In my Christian life, I run the race of faith. I do not struggle for the crown that I can receive. I strive to finish strong in my faith. GOD will make me a winner when I cross the finishing line. "Therefore, since we are surrounded by so great a cloud of witnesses, let us also lay aside every weight, and sin which clings so closely, and let us run with endurance the race that is set before us, looking to Jesus, the founder and perfecter of our faith, who for the joy that was set before him endured the cross, despising the shame, and is seated at the right hand of the throne of God. Consider HIM who endured from sinners such hostility against himself, so that you may not grow weary or fainthearted." (Hebrew 12:1-3).

In summary, Brethren, to win the Christian race; we must run with confidence, run with the right inspiration, and turn setbacks into comebacks. If we do these three things, we are on our way to winning the Christian race. Nonbelievers are not even in this Heaven's race. You have no hope of standing in the victory circle to receive your crown of life. You will be in the race only after you give your life to JESUS CHRIST THE REDEEMER. So, I would like to encourage you to give your life to the LORD today, by accepting HIM as your LORD and SAVIOUR, turn away from your wicked ways, repent from all righteousness, confessing your faith in JESUS and be baptized for the forgiveness of your sins. Life is like a race. Similarly, as believers, we work hard to fortify our faith to endure the race of faith. It is essential seek GOD daily by reading HIS word and in prayer. We must not abstain from fellowshipping with other believers to obtain encouragement in the faith. We must accept spiritual criticism and GODLY rebuke embrace trials. Individual chastisement is indispensable if we are to keep our eyes focused on JESUS.

**"The grass withers and the flowers fade,
But the word of our GOD stands forever."
(ISAIAH 40:8)**

CHAPTER 9

RAPTURE IS REAL

WHAT IS RAPTURE?

The word Rapture is not actually written in the Bible. Rapture means "grab" or "take away." The word Rapture is refer to the authentic believers being taken up to meet JESUS CHRIST with HIS Angels in the air as defined in this passage written by the apostle Paul: In (1st Thesollonian4:13-18) "But I would not have you to be ignorant, brethren, concerning them which are asleep, that ye sorrow not, even as others which have no hope. For if we believe that Jesus died and rose again, even so those who slept in Jesus will God bring with him. For this we say unto you by the word of the Lord, that we which are alive and remain unto the coming of the Lord shall not prevent them which are asleep. For the Lord himself shall descend from heaven with a shout, with the voice of the archangel, and with the trump of God: and the dead in Christ shall rise first: Then we which are alive and remain shall be caught up together with them in the clouds, to meet the Lord in the air: and so shall we ever be with the Lord" (1st Thesollonian4:13-18).

Wherefore comfort one another with these words" (1st Thessalonian 4:13-18), (KJV). Worries had risen during the Thessalonian Christians concerning the outcome of those Christians who had died before Christ returned. Would they miss the magnificent events of Christ's second coming and the resurrection? Paul guaranteed them in this way that God would save those who had before now died, as well as those still living. If this is the case, believers, are we ready for rapture? With the current events in all over the world, Jesus coming may not be far. According to the scripture, and things that are happening we know that His return will take place very soon. God is faithful to help us to the end. But the question for all of us is are we faithful enough to be rapture able? God does not want anything to deal with unstable Christians. He is a faithful God. Isaiah 41:10 "Fear thou not; for I am with thee: be not dismayed; for I am thy God: I will strengthen thee; yea, I will help yea, I will uphold thee with the right hand of my righteousness" (Isaiah 41:10).

> "The grass withers and the flowers fade,
> But the word of our GOD stands forever."
> (ISAIAH 40:8)

If we truly fear GOD and keep HIS laws, we will not have anything to fear about the rapture or the return of our LORD JESUS CHRIST. It is only if we are living a double standard life that we have everything to be concerned about. My prayer is that every soul should be rapture able. It is not the will of God that any soul should perish but that all should come to repentance. There are indications that we are in the period for the LORD to take His bride through rapture centered on what is happening on planet earth right now in connection to what the LORD spoke about in the bible about the end-times in relation to the rapture of the bride of Christ. Furthermore, based on what the spirit of the LORD reveals through prophesies, dreams, and manifestations etc., to His faithful children all over the world now.

The bible states that without Holiness no one will see God. Walking in Holiness means straightening yourself out of the worldly lifestyle and taking the narrow road where the presence of the LORD is and where the power of the Holy Spirit will guide you. It means surrendering your life for the LORD, and this may mean escaping the worldly behaviors like smoking, drinking fornicating etc. and living a life worthy of your calling of being a child of the LORD God Almighty (Jehovah Yahweh, I AM that I AM). A time in life will come when you must let go of some friends, family, lifestyles etc. that do not glorify the LORD since they may be a bad influence on your walk with the LORD of all LORDS.

The LORD wants us to completely surrender our life to Him. One leg out and one leg in is not accepted by the LORD of HOST, and those who live such a life are known as lukewarm Believers. We cannot serve two master's at the same time. In the book of Revelation chapter 3 the LORD says that He will spit such lukewarm Christians because they are neither warm nor cold (KJV). Brothers and sisters, it is necessary to completely surrender fully to the LORD and let Him take care and control of your life. There is everlasting blessing doing the will of God than doing it our own way. The LORD is only coming to take those who are expecting and watching for His return because in so doing they will be like the 5 wise virgins in the book of Mathew Chapter 25 who took time to fill their lamps with needed oil in preparation for the bridegroom because they made extra effort to be in the presence of the LORD in prayer, Righteousness, Repenting, Holiness, faithfulness, and fully surrender to the LORD Jesus Christ.

They were able to see the bridegroom when he came in. The other 5 foolish virgins were careless with their lifestyle, and they missed the mark. The same thing happened to Lot's wife when they were instructed to get out of Sodom and not to look back but somehow, she looked and became a pillar of salt up till this moment. Please let us be very careful with this race that is set before us. What He says He will do that will He do. **Jesus Christ** is coming

**"The grass withers and the flowers fade,
But the word of our GOD stands forever."
(ISAIAH 40:8)**

back. If we have not been living for HIM, we need to repent. Do not allow yourself to be misled. Do not forget that Jesus Christ and no-one else is the Lamb of God who paid all our debt on the Cross of Calvary by shedding His blood for our sin. Nourish on the word of God. Let the word of God be implanted on your heart. Place aside the things of this world that steal your heart. Think of what Jesus said, "In the world you will have tribulation, but be of good cheer, I have overcome the world."

In the early church time, the believers asked numerous questions about pre-tribulation rapture. In the writing of Apostle Paul in the book of Thessalonians chapter 2 he warned the Christians concerning the second coming of the Lord and our gathering together onto him. "Now we beseech you, brethren, by the coming of our Lord Jesus Christ, and by our gathering together unto him," 2 Thessalonians 2:1. Paul cautions the body of believers not to worry and explained to them things that must first happen before Jesus's coming. (In verses 2 and 3), It says, "That ye be not soon shaken in mind, or be troubled, neither by spirit, nor by word, nor by letter as from us, as that the day of Christ is at hand. ³ Let no man deceive you by any means: for that day shall not come, except there comes a falling away first, and that man of sin be revealed, the son of perdition."

What time is it Paul speaking about? He told us in verse one. "Believers gathering together unto HIM" (The Rapture). And Paul mentions that the son of Perdition or the man of sin must be revealed first, that would put us in the tribulation period. For those who say that the term man of sin does not necessarily mean it is the anti-Christ, The next verse describes the man of perdition as setting up himself to be worshiped. "Who opposeth and exalteth himself above all that is called God, or that is worshiped; so that he as God sitteth in the temple of God, shewing himself that he is God." I would say that is a correct description of the anti-Christ.

**"The grass withers and the flowers fade,
But the word of our GOD stands forever."
(ISAIAH 40:8)**

The dead in CHRIST will rise to meet HIM in the air. Will you be among them?

 **"The grass withers and the flowers fade,
But the word of our GOD stands forever."
(ISAIAH 40:8)**

CHAPTER 10

HEAVEN AND HELL ARE REAL

HEAVEN IS REAL: WHERE ARE YOU HEADING TO?
HELL, OR HEAVEN? THINK RIGHT!

GOD IS REAL. HEAVEN is real. Hell is real. Although many people these days are not sure that HEAVEN exists. The HOLY BIBLE made it clear that HEAVEN is real, and hell is also real. From the Book of Genesis to the Book of Revelation everything that the Bible said is true. The WORD OF GOD IS TRUE AND THEY ARE YE AND AMEN. Everything the Bible said that would happen is happening in our own very eyes. Many people do not believe that Heaven truly exists. But they reason that it may be simply an invention of people's imagination. Hebrews 9:23-2423; "It was therefore necessary that the patterns of things in the heavens should be purified with these; but the heavenly things themselves with better sacrifices than these; For CHRIST is not entered into the holy places made with hands, which are the figures of the true; but into heaven itself, now to appear in the presence of GOD for us:" The Word of GOD clearly declared that Heaven exists. It is a real place. The proceedings that happen there are real. God really is present there with the angels (HIS Divine Messengers). As children of God, Heaven will be our home too (John 14:2).

The writer of the book of Hebrews has written much about the holy places that GOD set up on this earth. But in Hebrews 8:5, the writer clarifies that those places were only duplicates. GOD set up those duplicates to communicate to HIS people about the truth. The truth is that the holy place is heaven. It is in heaven that GOD is present in all HIS glory. Glory means greatness. It defines the splendid and brilliant loveliness of GOD'S perfect character. To make the holy places on earth ready for use the blood of sacrifices became necessary. A gift that GOD considers valuable is a sacrifice. Here on earth, those sacrifices were animals. Nonetheless the blood of those animals was just a copy of the authenticity. The reality is in heaven. A better sacrifice was necessary there. That better sacrifice is the death of JESUS CHRIST, GOD'S SON. In GOD'S opinion nothing is more valuable than the blood of his own SON. JESUS' death happened on earth, of course. But then he went into the most holy place in heaven. And there, he offered his own blood to GOD the Father. Because GOD accepted the gift of JESUS' life, people can have a relationship with GOD. And all who become sons and daughters of the LIVING GOD will have a place in heaven.

**"The grass withers and the flowers fade,
But the word of our GOD stands forever."
(ISAIAH 40:8)**

Heaven or Hell - Which Will You Choose

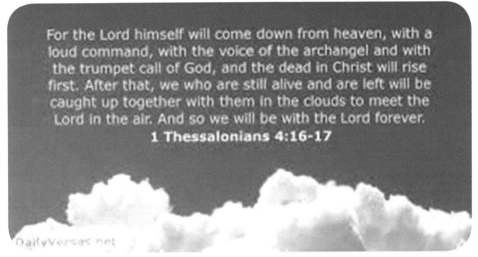

For the Lord himself will come down from heaven, with a loud command, with the voice of the archangel and with the trumpet call of God, and the dead in Christ will rise first. After that, we who are still alive and are left will be caught up together with them in the clouds to meet the Lord in the air. And so we will be with the Lord forever.
1 Thessalonians 4:16-17

DailyVerses.net

Friends, the year 2020 has been a difficult, painful, sorrowful, horror and grieving year for many worldwide. The year 2020 has taken over 5, 0000 (5 million) lives worldwide due to Coronal Virus- 19. In US alone over 500,000 souls died. I wonder where those that died are now spending eternity. Each day thousands of people take their last breath and slip into eternity, either into Heaven or into hell. The truth is that we may never know their individual names, the truth of death happens every day. What happens the moment after we die? The minute after we die, our soul provisionally leaves from our body to await the Resurrection. Those who place their faith in CHRIST will be carried by the angels into the presence of the LORD. They are now comforted.

Absent from the body and present with the Lord. Temporarily, non-believers await Hades for the final Judgment. "And in hell he lifts his eyes, being in torments... And he cried and said, Father Abraham, have mercy on me, and send Lazarus, that he may dip the tip of his finger in water, and cool my tongue; for I am tormented in this flame." (Luke 16:23a-24).

> **"The grass withers and the flowers fade,**
> **But the word of our GOD stands forever."**
> **(ISAIAH 40:8)**

"Then shall the dust return to the earth as it was: and the spirit shall return unto God who gave it." (Ecclesiastes 12:7). Even though we grieve over the loss of our loved ones, we are sorrowful, but not like those who have no hope. "For if we believe that JESUS died and rose again, even so them also which sleep in JESUS wills GOD bring with him. Then we, who are alive and remain shall be caught up with them in the clouds, to meet the LORD in the air: so, shall we ever be with the Lord? Wherefore comfort one another with these words." (1 Thessalonians 4:14, 17-18).

Although he cries in his torment, his prayer offers no comfort whatsoever, for a great gulf is fixed where no one can pass to the other side. Alone he is left in his misery. Alone in his memories. The flame of hope was forever extinguished on seeing his loved ones again. On the contrary, precious in the sight of the Lord is the death of HIM saints. Escorted by the angels into the presence of the LORD, they are now comforted. Their trials and suffering are past. Although their presence will be deeply missed, they have hope of seeing their loved ones again. Do you have the assurance that if you were to die today, you would be in the presence of the Lord in heaven?

Death for a believer is but a doorway that opens into eternal life. Those who fall asleep in Jesus will be reunited with their loved ones in heaven. Those you have laid in the grave in tears, you shall meet them again with joy! Oh, to see their smile and feel their touch never to part again. Friends, I am suggesting that you give your life to JESUS now while you still have opportunity to do so. But if you do not believe in the LORD JESUS CHRIST, you are going to hell. If you miss Heaven, you will not miss hell. There is no pleasant way I can say it. The word of GOD says, "For all have sinned, and come short of the glory of God." (Romans 3:23). Beloved, that includes you and me. Is only when we realize the dreadfulness of our sin against GOD and feel its deep sorrow in our hearts can we turn from the sin we once loved and accept the LORD JESUS as our SAVIOR. "That if thou shalt confess with thy mouth the LORD JESUS and shalt believe in thine heart that God hath raised him from the dead, thou shalt be saved." (Romans 10:9). Do not fall asleep without JESUS until you are assured of a place in heaven. It is not late to make things right with GOD to escape hell fire.

My friends do not wait any longer. Time waits for no one. Death is inevitable. Death can knock at your door in the next few minutes. You will not have the opportunity to say please come back let me make peace with anyone that I have bitterness or the individual that I hate so much. Let me make peace with my husband or my wife. It may be too late. Today is the day of salvation. Make things right while you still have your breath. For the coming back of JESUS CHRIST will be like a thief in the night. No man knows the time or the hour when the SON OF MAN will come back. Please do not miss this excellent opportunity to accept JESUS CHRIST as your LORD and SAVIOR. Doing this will grant you a place in HEAVEN to spend eternity with HIM forever.

**"The grass withers and the flowers fade,
But the word of our GOD stands forever."
(ISAIAH 40:8)**

You must ask for your sins to be forgiven and put your trust in the LORD. To be a believer in the LORD, ask for eternal life. There is only one way to heaven, and that is through THE LORD Today, if you would like to make JESUS THE LORD AND SAVIOR OF YOUR LIFE, and receive the gift of eternal life, please pray this prayer with me right now:

GIVE YOUR LIFE TO JESUS CHRIST. HE IS THE ONLY WAY TO GOD. That is GOD'S wonderful plan of salvation for HUMANITY AFTER THE FALL OF ADAM AND EVE.

You can begin a personal relationship with GOD by praying from your heart a prayer such as the following:

Dear LORD JESUS CHRIST:

- I recognize that you are the son of the HIGHEST GOD
- I am sorry for all the sins I have committed.
- Forgive me, LORD
- I trust you as my LORD.
- From this moment forward, LORD I surrender my life to you.
- I accept what you did for me in the CROSS of CALVARY
- You took my death penalty upon yourself.
- You covered my nakedness and took away my shame.
- From this day send I will live for you for the rest of my life
- So, help me JESUS MY LORD AND MY SAVIOUR
- Thank you for saving me LORD JESUS CHRIST
- IN JESUS NAME I PRAY AMEN.

Congratulations my friend, your name is now written in the book of life.

"So now there is no condemnation for those who belong to Christ Jesus. 2 And because you belong to him, the power [a] of the life-giving Spirit has freed you[b] from the power of sin that leads to death. 3 The law of Moses was unable to save us because of the weakness of our sinful nature. [c] So God did what the law could not do. He sent his own Son into a body like the bodies we sinners have. And in that body God declared an end to sin's control over us by giving his Son as a sacrifice for our sins. 4 He did this so that the just requirement of the law would be fully satisfied for us, who no longer follow our sinful nature but instead follow the Spirit" (Romans 8:1-4 NLT).

"The grass withers and the flowers fade,
But the word of our GOD stands forever."
(ISAIAH 40:8)

CHAPTER 11

HEAVEN AT LAST

Every Christian yearns for being raptured into the kingdom of heaven when JESUS returns. Bible verses about entering the kingdom of heaven will resolve your difficulties and problems about entering the kingdom of heaven. As we all know, there are many aspects of truth about entering the kingdom of heaven Christians must know, for example, how to enter the kingdom of heaven, the criteria for entering the kingdom of heaven, whether the kingdom of heaven is actually in heaven or on the earth, what kind of people can enter the kingdom of heaven, whether one can enter the kingdom of heaven through working hard for the Lord. Have you ever considered these questions seriously? If you want to resolve these problems and learn more truth about entering the kingdom of heaven, you can contact us via live chat. We will seek the truth about how Christians enter the kingdom of heaven with you as soon as possible, so that we can welcome the Lord at an early date and be raptured into the kingdom of heaven.

Christians often use the word heaven to refer to the final dwelling place of people who are saved. It is conceived as a place of perfection where people who have lived righteous lives will live eternally in God's presence.

Heaven (or heavens) has several meanings in the Bible. Physical heaven refers to the entire universe beyond earth (Genesis 1:1, Matthew 24:29, Revelation 12:3-4). "In my Father's house are many mansions: if it were not so, I would have told you. I will go to prepare a place for you. And if I go and prepare a place for you, I will come again and receive you to myself; that where I am, there you may be also" (John 14:2-3). "And God shall wipe away all tears from their eyes; and there shall be no more death, neither sorrow, nor crying, neither shall there be any more pain: for the former things are passed away" (Revelation 21:4). "And he showed me a pure river of water of life, clear as crystal, going ahead out of the throne of God and of the Lamb. In the middle of the street of it, and on either side of the river, there was the tree of life, which bore twelve manners of fruits, and yielded her fruit every month: and the leaves of the tree were for the healing of the nations. And there shall be no more curse: but the throne of God and of the Lamb shall be in it; and his servants shall serve him: And they shall see his face; and his name shall be in their foreheads. The grass withers and the flowers fade, But the word of our GOD stands forever." (ISAIAH 40:8)

"The grass withers and the flowers fade,
But the word of our GOD stands forever."
(ISAIAH 40:8)

And there shall be no night there; and they need no candle, neither light of the sun; for the Lord God gives them light: and they shall reign for ever and ever" (Revelation 22:1-5). Heaven is also the dwelling place of God (Deuteronomy 26:15, 1 Kings 8:28-30, Matthew 5:44-45).

When Christ returns, heaven and earth will be re-created or brought to perfection by God's will (Isaiah 65:17, 66:22, 2 Peter 3:10-13, Revelation 21:1). This new perfect world will be the final dwelling place for those who are saved (John 14:2-3, 1 Peter 1:3-4). Hades is a Greek word that is equivalent to the Hebrew Sheol. In the Greek version of the Old Testament, "Sheol" was translated as "Hades."In later Jewish writings, Sheol/Hades was conceived as having separate regions of comfort for the righteous and punishment of the wicked, and that idea is also seen in Jesus' Parable of the Rich Man and Lazarus: "The time came when the beggar died and the angels carried him to Abraham's side. The rich man also died and was buried. In Hades, where he was in torment, he looked up and saw Abraham far away, with Lazarus by his side. So, he called him, 'Father Abraham, have pity on me and send Lazarus to dip the tip of his finger in water and cool my tongue, because I am in agony in this fire.' "But Abraham replied, 'Son, remember that in your lifetime you received your good things, while Lazarus received bad things, but now he is comforted here and you are in agony" (Luke 16:22-26).

What Are Heaven And Hell Like?

The Bible does not give many details about either heaven or hell. The sayings in the Bible are often phrased in symbolic or figurative language. However, the Bible does make it clear that there will be a future glorious eternal life for the righteous and punishment for the wicked (Matthew 7:13-14, 13:40-42, 19:28-29, Luke 10:25-28, 13:24-28, John 5:28-29, 6:40, Romans 6:22-23, 8:18, Revelation 21:8). "When the Son of Man comes in his glory, and all the angels with him, then he will sit on the throne of his glory.

All the nations will be gathered before him, and he will separate people from one another as a shepherd separates the sheep from the goats, and he will put the sheep in his right hand and the goats at the left.

Then the king will say to those at his right hand, 'Come, you that are blessed by my Father, inherit the kingdom prepared for you from the foundation of the world; Then he will say to those at his left hand, 'You that are accursed, depart from me into the eternal fire prepared for the devil and his angels; And these will go away into eternal punishment, but the righteous into eternal life." (NRSV, Matthew 25:31-34, 41, 46). And I heard a loud voice from the throne

**"The grass withers and the flowers fade,
But the word of our GOD stands forever."
(ISAIAH 40:8)**

saying, "Look! God's dwelling place is now among the people, and he will dwell with them. They will be his people, and God himself will be with them and be their God. 'He will wipe every tear from their eyes. There will be no more death' or mourning or crying or pain, for the old order of things has passed away." (NIV, Revelation 21:3-4).

Many of our ideas about heaven and hell come from sources other than the Bible. The Divine Comedy, an epic poem written by Dante Alighieri in the 1300s, vividly describes hell, purgatory and heaven as imagined by Dante. Many of those ideas have endured to the present time. When Jesus comes again, all who have ever lived will be resurrected from the dead for a final judgment that decides their eternal fate. There is less certainty about what will happen in the intermediate state between the time of death and Jesus' second coming. The apostle Paul makes the analogy that our earthly bodies are like seeds that die and fall to the ground, then sprout into new, glorious forms of life (1 Corinthians 15:35-44). It is only an analogy, however. The Bible uses vague and poetic language to describe heaven, hell, and eternal life. The reason we know so few details about eternal life is that, as with other spiritual matters, the reality of it is simply beyond our human ability to comprehend. As Paul wrote,

Final Judgment & Resurrection of the Dead

The Last Judgment will occur after the resurrection of the dead and "our 'mortal body' will come to life again." Even those who profess Christianity will be judged by the deeds they have done in life when CHRIST comes again, there will be a resurrection of all the dead. Everyone, that is still living and the resurrected dead, will face God's judgment. Resurrection is the reuniting of the physical body and the spirit after death. The resurrection of the body is a subject of worldwide and profound standing. It challenges our cognitive powers, while it exalts our ideas of divine authority. With GOD, all things showed in HIS WORD are not only possible but convinced of accomplishment. The bodies of the saints, which are a part of the REDEEMER'S purchased, will be raised in Heavenly and wondrous faultlessness; like to the SAVIOUR'S GLORIOUS BODY.

In the Book of Isaiah, we were told by the prophet and repeated by the apostle. "Eye hath not seen, nor ear heard, neither have entered into the heart of man, the things which God hath prepared for them that love him" (Isaiah 64:4; 1st Corinthians 2:9). Not one iota of our dust can be lost; a cheerful, glorious expectation of the saints; but how earnest and terrible a thought to those who die without hope. Amongst Christians it is common to think and talk of the gladness of the Spirits of the just made perfect; but unfortunately, how infrequently do we think or speak of the perfect bliss of our entire nature, body, soul, and spirit incorruptible, unpolluted, glorified every part in the same way the object of the SAVIOUR'S purchase and of HIS care.

> **"The grass withers and the flowers fade,**
> **But the word of our GOD stands forever."**
> **(ISAIAH 40:8)**

As a child of GOD, I believe that the idea of everlasting life after death through the trust in CHRIST'S resurrection is a foundation of the Christian faith. Some Christian sects reflect the Second Coming of CHRIST to be the final and infinite judgment by GOD of the people of every nation following in the approval of some and the penalizing of others. The righteous will be granted eternal life; but the wicked will be condemned to eternal punishment. "Do not be amazed at this, for a time is coming when all who are in their graves will hear his [CHRIST'S] voice and come out - those who have done good will rise to live, and those who have done evil will rise to be condemned" (John 5:28-29).

God will judge different people by different standards, depending on their knowledge of the Gospel and the wealth, abilities and responsibilities that have been entrusted to them. "And I saw a great white throne, and him that sat on it, from whose face the earth and the heaven fled away; and there was found no place for them. And I saw the dead, small and great, stand before God; and the books were opened: and another book was opened, which is the book of life: and the dead were judged out of those things which were written in the books, according to their works. And the sea gave up the dead which were in it; and death and hell delivered up the dead which were in them: and they were judged every man according to their works. And death and hell were cast into the lake of fire.

This is the second death. And whosoever was not found written in the book of life was cast into the lake of fire" (Revelation 20:11-15). While we are still living, it is important surrender our life to JESUS while we have every opportunity to repent from our evil way (change our ways from evil to good). Nevertheless, in the end we will all be judged. Jesus said that we will be judged based on what we have done (or did not do) to help other people in need. But when the Son of Man comes in his glory, and all the angels with him, then he will sit upon his glorious throne. All the nations will be gathered in his presence, and he will separate the people as a shepherd separates the sheep from the goats. He will place the sheep in his right hand and the goats in his left.

"Then the King will say to those on his right, 'Come, you who are blessed by my Father, inherit the Kingdom prepared for you from the creation of the world. For I was hungry, and you fed me. I was thirsty, and you gave me a drink. I was a stranger, and you invited me into your home. I was naked, and you gave me clothing. I was sick, and you cared for me. I was in prison, and you visited me.' "Then these righteous ones will reply, 'Lord, when did we ever see you hungry and feed you? Or thirsty and give you something to drink? Or a stranger and show you hospitality? Or naked and give you clothing? When did we ever see you sick or in prison and visit you?' "And the King will say, 'I tell you the truth, when you did it to one of the least of these my brothers and sisters, you were doing it to me!'

"The grass withers and the flowers fade,
But the word of our GOD stands forever."
(ISAIAH 40:8)

"Then the King will turn to those on the left and say, 'Away with you, you cursed ones, into the eternal fire prepared for the devil and his demons. For I was hungry, and you did not feed me. I was thirsty, and you did not give me a drink. I was a stranger, and you did not invite me into your home. I was naked, and you did not give me clothing. I was sick and in prison, and you did not visit me.' "Then they will reply, 'Lord, when did we ever see you hungry or thirsty or a stranger or naked or sick or in prison, and not help you?' "And he will answer, 'I tell you the truth, when you refused to help the least of these my brothers and sisters, you were refusing to help me. "And they will go away into eternal punishment, but the righteous will go into eternal life." (NLT, Matthew 25:41-46)

The Apostle Paul Put It This Way:

Therefore, we are always confident and know that if we are at home in the body we are away from the Lord. We live by faith, not by sight. We are confident, I say, and would prefer to be away from the body and at home with the Lord. So, we make it our goal to please him, whether we are at home in the body or away from it. For we must all appear before the judgment seat of Christ, that each one may receive what is due him for the things done while in the body, whether good or bad. (NIV, 2 Corinthians 5:6-10)

What Kind Of People Can Enter Into Kingdom GOD?

What does the Bible talked to us about inheriting the kingdom GOD? This can only happen with those individuals whose righteousness surpasses the Scribes and Pharisees. This will only take place with people who truly and do the will of GOD. It is extremely difficult for a rich man. It is so vital, that it would be better to rip your eye out than to have two eyes and go to hell fire. It can take place only in those who are born of the Spirit. In addition, it can only take place through numerous tribulations. Obviously, entering the kingdom of GOD is tremendously important. It is the difference between spending eternity in Heaven or hell. It is significant that we should be willing to cut off our right hands or plug out right eyes, or go through challenging tribulations, give up our material wealth or money, do as we are told by JESUS CHRIST OUR REDEEMER, and practice righteousness to finally end up in the KINGDOM OF GOD. There are many quotes in the Scripture where CHRIST talked about the Kingdom of GOD.

**"The grass withers and the flowers fade,
But the word of our GOD stands forever."
(ISAIAH 40:8)**

What Does The Rest Of The Bible Say About Entering The KINGDOM Of GOD?

What kind of person will enter the kingdom? The LORD JESUS told us that only truthful people can enter the Kingdom of HEAVEN; only honest people can be people of the KINGDOM. The LORD JESUS' words tell us clearly that only those who do the will of the HEAVENLY FATHER can enter the KINGDOM OF HEAVEN. In the passages below, twice Jesus mentions the kingdom of God. Let us see what the LORD HIMSELF said about the Kingdom of GOD in the Book of Luke. "And they were even bringing their babies to Him so that He might touch them, but when the disciples saw it, they began rebuking them. But Jesus called for them, saying, "Permit the children to come to Me, and do not hinder them, for the kingdom of God belongs to such as these. Truly I say to you, whoever does not receive the kingdom of God like a child shall not enter it at all." (Luke 18:15-17). It is very clear now that from this passage that the kingdom of GOD belongs to a certain kind of individuals such as these.

We learn that we must receive the Kingdom, and we must enter the Kingdom. The Word of GOD made it clears to us what we as individuals needs to do to enter the Kingdom of GOD. CHRIST did not need so much from us. HE HIMSELF went through unspeakable agony to redeem us from the course of law. HE was treated as a criminal by me and you. The least we can do for HIM is to follow HIM to the core. It is for our own good if we follow CHRIST righteousness. Following HIS instructions will lead us to eternal life where we will spend eternity with HIM. Let us see what the LORD said about fake believers: "Not everyone that saith unto me, Lord, Lord, shall enter the kingdom of heaven; but he that doeth the will of my Father which is in heaven. Many will say to me on that day, Lord, Lord, have we not prophesied in thy name? and in thy name have cast out devils? and in thy name done many wonderful works? And then will I profess unto them, I never knew you: leave from me, ye that work iniquity" (Matthew 7:21-23).

JESUS said that some of the most improbable people would enter HIS Kingdom. But the big problem is that many religious people who do things in the name of CHRIST will not make it. They cannot give up believing in their own righteousness. Self-righteousness and religious pride can justify anything, even murder. Recall, religious leaders plotted to see JESUS crucified. The truth of the matter is that the only people who are qualified to go to heaven are the ones that do GOD'S will. The very nature of a Kingdom is that it glorifies its king. If our good works could get us into GOD'S kingdom, you know who would be taking the bows. It is human nature to love taking credit for us. The only people bowing in JESUS' kingdom will be those who fall on their faces to worship the KING OF KINGS and LORD OF LORDS.

"The grass withers and the flowers fade,
But the word of our GOD stands forever."
(ISAIAH 40:8)

Think about this my friends: Faith in JESUS CHRIST OF NAZERATH and HIS work on the cross is the **ONLY** tickets that will guarantee you to be a permanent resident in GOD'S kingdom. "For I say to you, that unless your righteousness surpasses that of the scribes and Pharisees, you shall not enter the kingdom of heaven." (Matthew 5:20). And Jesus said to His disciples, "Truly I say to you, it is hard for a rich man to enter the kingdom of heaven. And again, I say to you, it is easier for a camel to go through the eye of a needle, than for a rich man to enter the kingdom of GOD." (Matthew 19:23). "And if your eye causes you to stumble, cast it out; it is better for you to enter the kingdom of God with one eye, than having two eyes, to be cast into hell fire" (Mark 9:47). Jesus answered, "Truly, truly, I say to you, unless one is born of water and the Spirit, he cannot enter into the kingdom of God" (John 3:5). strengthening the souls of the disciples, encouraging them to continue in the faith, and saying, "Through many tribulations we must enter the kingdom of God" (Acts 14:22).

Friends in the LORD, the truth of the matter is that individual could agonize and sacrifice for spreading the Gospel our LORD and SAVIOR JESUS CHRIST; it is indisputable that they still often commit sins either sins of omission or commission. That individual sin confirms that they still have work to do to constantly have fellowship with GOD. We need to be aware that Satan is against us. This means that Satan is still at work to resist and betray GOD through us. How could those who resist God be qualified to enter the KINGDOM OF HEAVEN? No one can run the race without totally depending on CHRIST THE LORD. Remember no UNHOLY MAN OR WOMAN WILL ENTER THE KINGDOM OF GOD OR SEE GOD. Holiness can be obtained with THE GRACE AND MERCY OF GOD.

With constant fellowship with CHRIST, we shall scale any mountains. It is only sin that separates us from GOD. People can sacrifice for the LORD, spread the good news of CHRIS, build Churches/planting of Churches, and support Christians. These are all good individual behaviors. If their good behaviors are done for loving GOD, for truly working for GOD, and for obeying and satisfying GOD, without any thought of individual advance, these are truly good performances that will be remembered and be blessed by GOD. Nonetheless if their good performances are done for an exchange, for satisfying fleshly wants, or entering the KINGDOM OF HEAVEN and receiving rewards, then these good deeds are just deceptive in nature, and are against GOD! Could these deceiving behaviors be claimed to be following the HEAVENLY FATHER'S WILL? Could they be claimed to be holy? Unquestionably not! These decent behaviors are obsessed by their sinful nature and are demonstrations of exchange for privilege.

**"The grass withers and the flowers fade,
But the word of our GOD stands forever."
(ISAIAH 40:8)**

Some Scriptural Verses that can help us understand the topic about final judgement.

Matthew 5:29-30,
Matthew 10:28,
Matthew18:8-9,
Mark 9:43-48,
Luke 20: 45-47
Acts 24:15
John 9:40-41

Make out time to go through these passages to better understand the truth about GOD'S final judgement.

"The grass withers and the flowers fade,
But the word of our GOD stands forever."
(ISAIAH 40:8)

CHAPTER 12

HEAVEN IS A HOLY PLACE

"How Do I Prepare Myself For This Prepared Place Called HEAVEN?"

JUST TO GIVE US HEADS UP:

As we read the Holy Book of GOD, we find that HEAVEN is categorized as a place of rest and peace. It is a place invalid of suffering and death. It is a place of matchless beauty. It is a place where we will be forever united with our loved ones who slept in the LORD. To GOD is all the glory, HEAVEN is a place where we will dwell with the LORD JESUS during eternity. If we could imagine for a moment what HEAVEN is really like; we would not trade five minutes in HEAVEN for all of life on earth. JESUS said, "I have gone to prepare a place for you." We read in Matthew 25:34, "Then shall the King say unto them on his right hand, Come, ye blessed of my Father, inherit the kingdom prepared for you from the foundation of the world." a. Since JESUS is the One who created the Universe, HE has no problem in preparing a place for HIS saints. The Apostle Paul wrote in Col. 1:16, "For by him were all things created, that are in heaven, and that are in earth, visible and invisible, whether they be thrones, or dominions, or principalities, or powers: all things were created by him, and for him."

"Let not your heart be troubled: believe in God, believe also in me. In my Father's house are many mansions; if it were not so, I would have told you; for I go to prepare a place for you. And if I go and prepare a place for you, I will come again and receive you unto myself; that is where I am, there you may be also. And whither I go, you know the way. Thomas says to him, "Lord, we know not whither you go; how know we the way? Jesus says to him, I am the way, and the truth, and the life: no one comes unto the Father, but by me. If you had known me, you would have known my FATHER also: from henceforth you have known him and have seen him. Philip says to him, Lord, show us the Father, and it suffices for us. JESUS says to him, Have I been so long time with you, and do you not know me, Philip? he that has seen me has seen the Father; how say you, Show us the Father? Believe you not that I am in the FATHER, and the FATHER in me? the words that I say to you I speak not from myself; but the FATHER abiding in me does his works. Believe me that I am in the FATHER, and the FATHER in me: or else believe me for the very works' sake" (John 14:1-11).

In just four verses, Romans 12:1-4, we learn that GOD will one day set up a new heaven and a new earth. GOD is making all things new. If we think this world is good, we have not seen anything yet. Something better than all we can dream or envisage is on the horizon. Just think that every tear you and I have shed, for any reason, will be wiped away by the GOD of HEAVEN.

**"The grass withers and the flowers fade,
But the word of our GOD stands forever."
(ISAIAH 40:8)**

Then comes the most profound thought of all GOD HIMSELF will be with us. We will dwell in the presence of ALL AND MIGHTY GOD forever.

I believe this will be heaven at its absolute best. I love cherishing the words of 1 John 5:11-13. "GOD has given us eternal life, and this life is in HIS SON. HE who has the Son has life; he who does not have the Son of GOD does not have life. I write these things to you who believe in the name of the Son of GOD so that you may know that you have eternal life." Heaven is a prepared place for prepared people. Have you prepared to be with your HEAVENLY FATHER throughout eternity? I believe you have done so and are continually working on it! JESUS makes it possible for all of us to spend eternity with HIM in Heaven. My brothers and sisters, I want to be ready for that day. We should not miss Heaven for crying aloud. Do not miss it! With JESUS in the vessel, we shall smile at the storm of life.

Holiness is our criteria to HEAVEN:

Holiness means being distinct set apart from everything that does not give glory to GOD. Any action of ours that will separates us from GOD. Avoiding sin will lead us to holiness. Christians are holy people in two ways. First, believers are holy in God's sight in terms of their position. Through faith in Christ, they are uniquely set apart by God, and for God. In this sense, no true Christian can be any more holy than he already is. When a Christian gives his or her life to JESUS CHRIST, he or she is new creature old things are passed away and all things become new. Christ transforms us to HIS image. We become little CHRIST in our daily life. This includes every area of our existence. The Word of GOD that is the Bible also speaks of the need for consistent and increasing holiness in behavior. As a result, the holy person practices righteousness rather than sin, lives in cleanliness rather than uncleanness, is GODLY rather than worldly.

CONSIDER FOUR FACTS FROM THE BIBLE ABOUT HOLINESS IN BEHAVIOR:

Holiness Is Not Optional:

"Pursue peace with all men, and the sanctification [or "holiness"] without which no one will see the Lord" (Heb. 12:14). The two commands in this verse may initially appear to conflict with each other: have a good relationship with all people and be holy in your behavior. If we allow peace with the people of this world to be our overriding concern, we might easily be negligent in living according to God's standard of holiness. The practice of holiness has the tendency to offend. So, the writer saw the need to be suitable in his first command with a second: be holy in your conduct even if it causes conflict with others. I tend to believe that the reason for giving the second command precedence over the first is seen in the last phrase: "without which [i.e., without holiness] no one will see the Lord."

**"The grass withers and the flowers fade,
But the word of our GOD stands forever."
(ISAIAH 40:8)**

You may complete your life, as many Christian martyrs did, as the apostles did, and as JESUS HIMSELF did, among great hostility from most people around you, and still be self-assured of your entrance into heaven. However, if you die as one whose behavior was not consistently and increasingly holy not set apart from the worldliness all around you then as this text makes plain, you will not "see the Lord." Instead, you will hear, "I never knew you. Depart from Me, you who practice lawlessness" (Matt. 7:23).

In Every Angle Of Our Life Holiness Is Required:

Some of us that have children want our children to be us anywhere or in any corner; they must preserve and represent the image of the family. Anything less than this will create friction between parents and the children. Obedient children will always be loved by their parents. They behaved well and conformed to their parents' instructions. So, why can't we honor and obey GOD when HE said we should be holy as HE is Holy? Our expectation from us is for us to be holy. Parents also need to live a life of holiness. We are mandated to be holy in our behavior and in everything we do; because it is written, "You shall be holy, for I am holy." (1 Pet. 1:14-16).

Take notice about the words, "in all our behavior." In this manuscript, Christian liberty has its border. We are free to live as we want to live and do as we want to do if all our behavior is holy. And by holy, Peter undoubtedly directs us to emulate GOD. Would GOD approve of the things we allow ourselves to do, say, think, listen to, or watch? In our unawareness as a nonbeliever, we felt no doubt about engaging in less-than-holy behavior. But what about here and now, as one who has been set apart for GOD? Are we pursuing holiness in every area, or are there still dark corners of our life where we are taking freedoms we should not?

The SWORD OF THE SPIRIT Is The Only Instruction Manual For Holiness:

During our school days be it Elementary or High school or Colleges or Universities, our instructors or professors have an expectation of all their students. No matter how smart one is you still must read to understand what you are expected to know for the subject. So, it is with Christians. We cannot achieve holiness without reading the Bible. I do not mean just reading the Bible as if is ordinary book. We need to study the Bible make notes ask questions from older saints or your pastors or your ministers for a detailed explanation. Just like you go to your teacher for an explanation of unclear area of your subject. The Psalmist inquires a humble yet deep question: "How can a young man keep his way pure?" (Ps. 119:9). This was no mirror image of lazy inquisitiveness, but rather an expression of crucial need and belief. The Psalmist wanted to be pure (holy, righteous) in the way he led his life, and so he asked how this could be done. He then gave the only acceptable answer: "By keeping it according to Your word."

**"The grass withers and the flowers fade,
But the word of our GOD stands forever."
(ISAIAH 40:8)**

Holiness is not the invention of instinct, but of instruction. The person who walks in holiness is the one who knows and reads and obeys his Bible. My friends read your Bible daily and the HOLY SPIRIT OF GOD will direct you and teach on which way to follow. Reading the Bible consistently is the gateway to Holiness. GOD will reward you for obeying HIS word and command. The practice of holiness is the same as a vigorous spiritual life. A person cannot have one without the other, and the person who has the one also has the other. Both flow from one's relationship with Scripture. According to Muller, G. a 19th century man of GOD, said, "the vigor of our spiritual life will be in exact proportion to the place held by the Bible in our life and thoughts."

My dear brothers, sisters, and friends, in conclusion of being Holy, after you have done everything stand. Do not be discouraged, ashamed, or embarrassed if people around you make mockery for you for being holy. We should keep holiness because it is needed from us as children GOD. Apostle Paul wrote after he had suffered a lot for CHRIST sake, he was so much that I strongly believe that his reward in Heaven will be great. He stood firm for the propagation of the Gospel of JESUS CHRIST. He said, "For I am now ready to be offered, and the time of my departure is at hand. I have fought a good fight, I have finished my course, I have kept the faith: Henceforth there is laid up for me a crown of righteousness, which the Lord, the righteous judge, shall give me at that day: and not to me only, but unto all them also that love his appearing" (2 Timothy 4:6-8). In a real sense, how can many comfortably say this today that majority of believers have become cowards? We hear the word of GOD every time and yet there is no change in our behavior or see manifestation of the power of HOLY SPIRIT OF GOD IN OUR LIFE. There must be a transformation in our life if we really have surrender all to GOD.

Autonomy Of Choice Involves Holiness!

Apostle Paul in his writing to the believers in Rome mentioned to the Christians to take pains to avoid even being tempted to sin. "Make no provision for the flesh in regard to its lusts" (Rom. 13:14). This is a command to exercise the will to recognize the seductive, deceptive nature of sin and the unholy wishes of your flesh that still tend to draw you toward sin, and then to make every effort to keep the two away from each other. If you want to avoid a deadly explosion, you will keep open blazes away from petrol vapor. Similarly, if you want to avoid sinning, you will be careful to avoid unnecessarily placing ourselves in the presence of temptation.

If our only command were to avoid committing the sin itself, there would be no defilement in simply drawing near, if we did not actually yield. But with Paul's command in Romans 13:14, we sin when we become inconsiderate. The choice is yours and

> **"The grass withers and the flowers fade,**
> **But the word of our GOD stands forever."**
> **(ISAIAH 40:8)**

mine. Do not be confirmed to this world. Let the JOY OF THE LORD be your strength. Remember we are mandated to brighten the corners where we are always. Holiness requires carrying your cross every day if we have breath in us.

"The grass withers and the flowers fade,
But the word of our GOD stands forever."
(ISAIAH 40:8)

CHAPTER 13

HEAVEN IS ONLY FOR HOLY PEOPLE

At this end time, many people both Christians and non-Christians not long believe in being holy. Holiness is a thing of old. GOD demands us to be holy just as HE is holy. It is Holiness or hell. Do not allow fake prophets to deceive you or seduce you. Whatever that will please GOD according to the Bible do it. It is for your own good. No one can quench the fire in hell. According to the word of GOD, it is a place of no turning back. Hell is a place of no return. No opportunity to repent in hell. You have opportunity now to repent and make things right with GOD. No repentance in the grave either.

You do not want to be burning in hell fire with those fake believers and their master devil and his agents whose job was to deceive and discourage believers on earth from following CHRIST in the Spirit and in Truth. Today is the day of Salvation. Get away from those of them that despise the Gospel of JESUS CHRIST. Only holy people are found in HEAVEN. It is so foolish and crazy how people who claim to love GOD and think they are filled with the Holy Ghost just because they can speak in tongues, but they literally despise GOD'S heart and who HE is - Holy. No man or woman will miss hell without a heart of obedience to the holiness of JESUS CHRIST.

Time has come for some of these fake preachers to stop the drama at the pulpit and get down to the business of the Gospel of JESUS CHRIST. Ability does not fly in the kingdom of GOD, and when we value ability more than we value holiness, it just proves we really do not know GOD at all. Hell is going to have a lot of surprise guests. This is true because the word of GOD said so. "Not everyone that saith unto me, Lord, Lord, shall enter the kingdom of heaven; but he that doeth the will of my Father which is in heaven. Many will say to me on that day, Lord, Lord, have we not prophesied in thy name? and in thy name have cast out devils? and in thy name done many wonderful works? And then will I profess unto them, I never knew you: leave from me, ye that work iniquity" (Matt 7:21-23).

The dictionary defines holiness as being free from sin. In Hebrews 12:14, "Follow peace with all men and holiness, without which no man can see God." (Hebrews 12:14). Many in the body of CHRIST are blindly going along believing none can live Holy today. They claim that because of what is currently going on the planet earth, "It is not possible to live Holy in this life anymore." But GOD has not changed. Heaven and hell are still there. What did the word of GOD say: "That he would grant unto us, that we are being delivered out of the hand of our enemies might serve him without fear, in holiness and righteousness before him, all the days of our life." (Luke 1:74-75).

According to this scripture we are to live holy right here in this life. If we have these words, "For the grace of GOD that bringeth salvation hath appeared to all men, teaching us that denying ungodliness and worldly lusts, we should live soberly, righteously, and godly, in this

> **"The grass withers and the flowers fade,**
> **But the word of our GOD stands forever."**
> **(ISAIAH 40:8)**

present world." (Titus 2:11-12). In everything we do or say we are to live holy. "But as HE which hath called you is holy, so be ye holy in all manner of conversation; because it is written; 'Be ye holy; for I am holy.'"(1 Peter 1:15-16).

There is such a great need for holy conversation today among religious people. Sometimes you cannot believe what comes out our mouth as Christians. "For even hereunto were ye called, because Christ also suffered for us, leaving us an example, that ye should follow in his steps: Who did not sin, neither was guile found in his mouth." (1st Peter 2:21-22). Living holy in Christ Jesus means simple living free from sin. The Apostle Paul writes, "Awake to righteousness and sin not." (1st Corinthians 15:34). God's standard is "SIN NOT" Look at John 8:11. Jesus speaks these words, "Go and sin no more." Then in John 5:14 we find Jesus talking to the crippled man that was healed, he said, "Sin no more, lest a worse thing come unto thee. Bear in mind that the Holy Ghost has not come yet.

Surely if those people before us were able to live free from sin without the HOLY GHOST, we ought to be able to live free from sin with the help of the HOLY GHOST. "My little children, these things write I unto you that ye sin not. And if any man sin, we have an advocate with the Father, JESUS CHRIST the righteous" (1st John 2:1). In verse 6 of this same chapter, He says, "He that saith he abideth in HIM ought himself also to walk, even as HE walked." Peter tells us in 1 Peter 2:21-22 how he walked. Without guile and without sin. Paul in 2nd Tim. 2:19 say "Let everyone that nameth the name of Christ departs from iniquity." It seems very clear from these scriptures that GOD requires a sinless life. "What shall we say then? Shall we continue in sin, that grace may abound?" GOD forbid. How shall we that are dead to sin, live any longer therein? (Romans 6:1-2).

Love Of Money, Lust Of The Eyes, Lust Of The Flesh, And Pride Of Life

Friends, disobedience are a serious sin against GOD. When we go through the BIBLE, we see that those who disobeyed GOD did not have it easy. If in doubt, go ask King Saul, Achan, Ghazi, etc. The truth is that those who love money more than GOD, have lust of the eyes, lust of the flesh, and have pride of life, will not inherit the Kingdom of GOD. This iniquity caused satan to fall from a place of worshipping GOD to a place of using wisdom for himself in disobedience to GOD. Satan also used it to get Eve to convince Adam to disobey GOD.

He told Eve she would be wise in disobedience, and Eve lusted after the beauty and taste of the fruit. The antidote for iniquity is GOD'S grace (favor AND power to obey), which leads to holiness (separation to GOD'S purposes away from lust and pride), obedience, humility and

**"The grass withers and the flowers fade,
But the word of our GOD stands forever."
(ISAIAH 40:8)**

dependence on GOD. I hope that clears things up. God is patient, so you do not have to fear HIS wrath. But HIS grace is powerful, and you should be constantly growing in it the more contact you have with HIM. The Bible exhorts us to examine ourselves, to see whether we are really in the faith. Nothing is better or more pleasurable than GOD, so there is no reason to fall short of HIS grace.

Now unto him that can keep you from falling, and to present you faultless before the presence of his glory with exceeding joy, To the only wise God our SAVIOUR, be glory and majesty, dominion, and power, both now and ever" (Jude 1:22-25). The truth is that several of us are not comfortable in discussing what will happen once we transit out of this world. Even though it is not a widely held topic of discussion, the assumption that most of us just tell ourselves that after we die, we will go to heaven. Unfortunately, this may be nothing more than a coping mechanism to avoid facing the hard truth.

Consequently, according to the HOLY BOOK, THE BIBLE, does each one of us qualify everyone go to HEAVEN after we die? While every person can go to heaven after they die, not everyone will spend eternity there. According to the HOLY BIBLE, heaven is a place where people who have put their trust in JESUS CHRIST will spend eternity with HIM. If you choose to reject or deny your need for Savior, you will not receive the great gift of eternal life in heaven. The HOLY BOOK, THE BIBLE made it clear that the gift of an eternity in HEAVEN is the ultimate gift. Everyone has access to this gift of salvation. It is available to anyone who accepts JESUS CHRIST AS THEIR LORD AND SAVIOR, repents of their sins, and places their trust in GOD.

Is Heaven A Real Place?

Brothers, sisters, and friends, contrary to what many people believe, HEAVEN is not just a physical place or just a fairytale. Some of us are skeptical as to whether heaven is really an existing place. Heaven is, in fact, a very real place. It is a peaceful place, packed of the GLORY of GOD. In HEAVEN, believers will spend eternity worshipping their SAVIOR THE LION OF THE TRIBE OF JUDA; THE USPRING OF DAVID and delighting in HIS presence throughout eternity. Will you not like to be there where there will be no night, no death, no sickness, no sorrow, no pains, and JESUS CHRIST WILL REIGN AS THE ONLY KING FOREVER. There will be no more tears and weeping for the LORD HIMSELF will wipe away all our tears.

**"The grass withers and the flowers fade,
But the word of our GOD stands forever."
(ISAIAH 40:8)**

Based on the research in the Scriptures, I found several evidence that we can learn about HEAVEN throughout the HOLY BOOK: the BIBLE. You can find true evidence in the following part of the Scripture:

- Heaven is God's dwelling place. (Psalm 33:13)

- Heaven is paradise. (Luke 23:43)

- Heaven is known as the Father's House. (John 14:2)

- Heaven is where Christ currently dwells. (Acts 1:11)

- Christians go to Heaven when they die. (Philippians 1:21-23)

OUR HEAVELY FATHER, THE HOLY ONE OF ISRAEL, has graciously given us understanding into the glory that waits for us upon transitory from this life. Nevertheless, because of the magnificence of HEAVEN, we could not even start to understand its reality.

**"The grass withers and the flowers fade,
But the word of our GOD stands forever."
(ISAIAH 40:8)**

⚜

C H A P T E R   1 4

ESCAPE GOD'S FINAL JUDGEMENT

What Did the WORD of GOD Say About GOD'S Judgment? The Bible made it clear that GOD is a righteous Judge. GOD is not respecter of any person. It is clear in the WORD of GOD that sin will result in internal condemnation and righteousness will lead to internal life. GOD has continuously been as judge over HIS creation. Nonetheless we need to know how HE judges when GOD judges and why HE judges. It is imperative to understand how, at what time and why HE judges aid us to understand the kinds of judgment defined in the Bible. As soon as GOD determined to judge Sodom and Gomorrah for their sins, Lots uncle Abraham acknowledged that GOD is the judge of HIS creation's actions (Genesis 18:20-25). In this case GOD passed judgment, issued a verdict, and passed out the sentence.

GOD will JUDGE the WORLD in RIGHTEOUSNESS.
Acts 17:31

"The grass withers and the flowers fade,
But the word of our GOD stands forever."
(ISAIAH 40:8)

In Psalms 75:7, "But God is the Judge; He puts down one, and exalts another. King Nebuchadnezzar came to recognize this (Daniel 4:37), and Daniel passed on this truth to the blasphemous Belshazzar (Daniel 5:21-22).

GOD mandates us to be Holy. Again no unholy person will see GOD. This is the time to make things right with GOD. Night is coming when no one will be able to work. No repentance inside the grave. Make the use of your time now to accept JESUS CHRIST as your LORD and SAVIOR. My wish for anyone who is reading this book is to be ready because there is no time to change your mind when CHRIST will come to take HIS OWN people.

**"The grass withers and the flowers fade,
But the word of our GOD stands forever."
(ISAIAH 40:8)**

GOD is the righteous Judge over all HIS creation, and HE makes all decisions. It is in HIS power to decide and conduct-RIGHTEOUS AND MERCIFUL JUDGMENTS. We can be confident that GOD is a righteous judge (Psalms 7:11; 2 Timothy 4:8). Judgment of GOD is not delivered on many of the people now in this age for the purpose of eternal salvation. This judgment of GOD will occur later. The book of Jude tells us that "the Lord comes with ten thousands of His saints to execute judgment on all" (Jude 1:14-15). Friends are you ready for this final judgement of GOD? More so, the judgement of GOD will begin in the house of GOD. King David saw GOD'S judgments in all His works and recognized that they were clear all over the creation (Psalms 105:5, 7). David knew all GOD'S decisions concerning him were right and in his finest interest. Therefore, King David praised GOD repeatedly for HIS faithful judgments in his life (Psalms 119:20; Psalms 119:62; Psalms 119:75).

The ultimate purpose GOD for man that HE made in HIS image is that he will enjoy eternal life in the family of his Ageless GOD. The final judgement of GOD is not now. HE is giving us the opportunity to repent and do the right thing that will prevent us from HIS end time judgement. For instance, Peter mentioned to us that "the time has come for judgment to begin at the house of God" (1 Peter 4:17). At this point, we can see that judgment is an assessment procedure that has at present began for those who are a part of GOD'S CHURCH-"the house of GOD." This assessment in the end leads to the execution of a decision or judgment. During the Millennium, every one of us will be held accountable when GOD will judge people on how they live during that time; the period 1,000 years (Revelation 20:4).

We will all be judged according to our work after this evaluation process, (Revelation 22:12). There will be a reckoning after only an unbiased and sufficient process is complete (Matthew 25:31-34; Matthew 25:46). When you really turn to God, you can confidently ask HIM to step into your life in a powerful way. How GOD deals with you to fulfill HIS purpose in you is described in the Bible as a form of HIS "judgments." When GOD is intimately involved in your life, He makes decisions about you daily. HIS decisions about us have to do with answers to our prayers, bestowing His blessings on us, protecting us and even allowing us to endure trials. God is deeply interested in us and how we are progressing toward fulfilling HIS purpose.

**"The grass withers and the flowers fade,
But the word of our GOD stands forever."
(ISAIAH 40:8)**

CONCLUSION

....

Dear brothers and sisters, it is true that I am authoring a book on **the PURSUIT OF HOLINESS INSTEAD OF PURSUIT OF HAPPINESS.** I am the least qualified individual to author a book on holiness or talk about holiness. I was just obeying what the HOLY SPIRIT of GOD dropped in my heart during my quite time in the morning few years ago. Writing this has challenged me to be mindful of my walk with GOD. Since I started authoring this book, I now have the mindset of the Kingdom of GOD. My perspective on the Heavenly race has dramatically changed. The Book of Hebrew scared me to death: "Work at living in peace with everyone, and work at living a holy life, for those who are not holy will not see the Lord." (Hebrew 12:14). I have told myself that whatever it takes to keep a life of holiness I will try to do it by the special grace and mercy of GOD ONLY.

It will be terrible of this noise that we are Christians but on the judgment day we find ourselves in a wrong side, GOD FORBID. It will never be our part IJMN AMEN. With this concept, HOLINESS BECOMES DO OR DIE AFAIRS. We must speak to ourselves daily that we must live a holy life. "There was a man named Jabez who was more honorable than any of his brothers. His mother named him Jabez because his birth was so painful. 10 He was the one who prayed to the GOD of Israel, "Oh, that you would bless me and expand my territory! Please be with me in all that I do and keep me from all trouble and pain!" And GOD granted him his request." (1st Chronicles 4:9-10). Jabez changed his destiny. Anyone of us can change that ugly stigma that the devil puts on us. OUR GOD IS IN CONTROL OF OUR LIFE.

The body of CHRIST should make every effort to be holy; without holiness no one will see the LORD. If we want to see GOD, all of us should aspire to be holy. Just like Christian race is an individual determination, being holy is also an individual decision or determination.

Compared to the holiness of GOD, the idea of being Holy can seem very distant and difficult to get to. It is not easy at all. But by the grace and mercy of GOD it can be attainable.

Siblings, whether we like it or not, we are called to be holy, that fact cannot be avoided. This will not just be an Old Testament concept that is swept away in the New Testament the Old Testament exhortation to holiness (Leviticus 11:44) is repeated and even amplified in Peter's letter. The impression of holiness appears intimidating or dreadful to us.

Everyone that calls himself or herself a child of GOD knows that Holiness is absence of sin. What comes to our mind most of the time when we talk about holiness is its virtuously negative aspect: the absence of sin. "Those who have been born into God's family do not make a practice of sinning, because God's life[a] is in them. So, they cannot keep on sinning, because they are children of GOD. Our actions will show that we belong to the truth, so we will be confident when we stand before GOD." (1st John 3: 9 and 1st John 5:19).

The point I am trying to make here is that when we become Christians, transformation takes place in our life. Something significant changes within us when we give our lives to CHRIST "If anyone is in Christ, he is a new creation" (2nd Corinthians 2:17). God changes our inner selves so that sin is no longer natural or inevitable for us as it was before we became Christians.

In his letter to the brethren in Rome Apostle Paul wrote: "What shall we say then? Shall we continue in sin, that grace may abound? God forbid. How shall we, that are dead to sin, live any longer therein?" (Romans 6:1-2).

- Holiness is an absence of sin.
- Spiritual completeness
- Set apart for GOD (Daniel set himself apart for GOD)

 **"The grass withers and the flowers fade,
But the word of our GOD stands forever."
(ISAIAH 40:8)**

We fight a clever adversary and must be prepared with the full armor of God to stand firm against Him

THE ARMOR OF GOD

EPHESIANS 6:10-18
"... Be strong in the Lord and in his mighty power. Put on the full armor of God so that you can take your stand against the devil's schemes." v. 10, 11

The Shield of Faith (Eph. 6:16)
Faith is being sure that God will keep His promises. Faith in God protects you when you are tempted to doubt.

The Helmet of Salvation (Eph. 6:17)
Put on the Helmet of Salvation by believing that Jesus Christ died for your sins and rose again.

The Breastplate of Righteousness (Eph. 6:14)
Righteousness is being honest, good, humble, and fair to others. It means standing up for weaker people.

The Belt of Truth (Eph. 6:14)
Truth keeps us from giving in to the world's beliefs. Compare your beliefs and actions to the truth of the Word of God.

The Sword of the Spirit (Eph. 6:17)
which is the Word of God. God's Word is our offensive weapon. When we tell others what the Bible says, the Holy Spirit helps people see their bad thoughts and actions, and makes them want to be forgiven.

Feet Prepared with the **Gospel of Peace** (Eph. 6:15)
The Gospel of Peace is being right with God and being contented in troubled times. Jesus said peacemakers were blessed.

"The grass withers and the flowers fade,
But the word of our GOD stands forever."
(ISAIAH 40:8)

"The grass withers and the flowers fade,
But the word of our GOD stands forever."
(ISAIAH 40:8)

CHAPTER 15

USA! WHERE ARE YOU AS A NATION? "IN PURSUIT OF HOLINESS?"

For many years, United States of America prosperity, technology, and scientific advancements have exceeded all preceding civilizations. It is believed that this nation has enjoyed GOD'S divine blessing because many of the Pilgrims and the Founding Fathers sought after the counsel of GOD'S WORD as they forged our national identity (Psalm 33:12). Drawing from this inheritance, the United States has drove world missions, make friends with the Jewish people, and encouraged liberty and justice. Opponents of Christianity can try to redraft our country's heritage; on the other hand, they will fail. United States of America's identity is bound up in its faith. USA needs to continuously keep Holiness in our governmental system, churches, communities, and in our homes. Holiness has no limits to pastors or ministers only. Holiness is for everyone including the President, vice president, Senators, Congress, Governors, Mayors, Alderman, men and women in the military, Police Officers, and citizens. There is moral decay right now in our blessed country.

If this wonderful foundation is allowed to corrode, it will come at a sheer cost. The story of the earlier world powers for example Greece, Babylon, and Rome proposes that the utmost threats to USA have yet to come lie within. Earlier kingdoms followed a development something like this: they stimulated oppression to spiritual faith; from faith to audacity; from bravery to freedom; from freedom to plenty; from profusion to satisfaction; from satisfaction to indifference; from indifference to dependence; and from dependence back to slavery. Our great nation can imagine a dissimilar future if it exchanges the PURSUIT of HOLINESS/ GODLINESS for worthless things like apathy, immorality, and greediness. The Bible warns of three national sins that result in GOD turning HIS back on a nation. GOD mandated all of us to live a holy and a righteous life. This mandate came directly from the Word of GOD, not the world or the government.

UNGRATEFULNESS:

America should not be ungrateful to GOD'S faithfulness to them as a nation. According to the book of Judges, Israel pedaled through revolt, retribution, repentance, and restoration thirteen times. Far ahead, the prophet Jeremiah reminded the people Israel of how close they had been to the LORD when the nation was set up (Jeremiah 2:1-2). Jeremiah warned the children of Israel that their insensitivity would suffer God's judgment, and it did. If America hopes to enjoy GOD'S continued blessing, it will do well to pay attention to Jeremiah's warning with a grateful heart. National holiness becomes imperative for everyone both old and young, poor, and rich. This present generation do not care about GOD and HIS WORD.

> **"The grass withers and the flowers fade,
> But the word of our GOD stands forever."
> (ISAIAH 40:8)**

INSIGNIFICANCE:

In what way did Israel answer to GOD'S assessment? According to Book of Jeremiah 2:6-8; Neither did they say, 'Where is the Lord, Who brought us up out of the land of Egypt,

**"The grass withers and the flowers fade,
But the word of our GOD stands forever."
(ISAIAH 40:8)**

Who led us through the wilderness, Through a land of deserts and pits, Through a land of drought and the shadow of death, Through a land that no one crossed And where no one dwelt?'

7 I brought you into a bountiful country, To eat its fruit and its goodness. But when you entered, you defiled My land And made My heritage an abomination. 8 "The priests did not say, 'Where is the Lord?' And those who handled the law did not know Me; The rulers also transgressed against Me; The prophets prophesied by Baal And walked after things that do not profit" (Jeremiah 2:6-8 NKJV).

IDOLATRY:

This is what the LORD says: "What did your ancestors find wrong with me that led them to stray so far from me? They worshiped worthless idols, only to become worthless themselves (Jeremiah 2:5). I believe that GOD ALMIGHTY possibly will ask the same question of United State of America. Why has the most blessed nation on earth turned its back on GOD in favor of self-centeredness? Disorder, divisions, and economic struggles have replaced GOD'S harmony and provision because we have pushed GOD from the public square to the sideline of our nation's life.

Even the Church in America has allowed moral belief to dictate how it expresses its faith. Consequently, the Church is misplacing its significance. CHRIST calls us "the light of the world" (Matthew 5:14), but HE has also warned that HE will remove our lampstand our influence if we stray from HIM and do not repent (Revelation 2:4-5). Our mandate for righteous living comes from the Word of God, not the world. America needs to come back to GOD and cry for forgiveness and mercy. The land of our nation can no longer have the innocent blood that is poured into it every single second, from the mother's womb to the shooting on the street. There is moral decay in this blessed nation. America comes back to GOD. HE IS GOD OF TRILLION CHANCES. The Book of Proverbs 14:34 says, "Godliness makes a nation great, but sin is a disgrace to any people" (NLT). "He will guard the feet of his faithful ones, but the wicked shall be cut off in darkness, for not by might shall a man prevail." (1st Samuel 2:9; ESV). It is important for us to repent and totally give ourselves to GOD HE will have mercy on us.

For this nation to continue to enjoy the goodness of GOD, everyone needs to make a U-turn. Tracing our way back to GOD is an antidote from heading to destruction. There are no other ways to be at peace with GOD than to call for national repentance and deliverance. We need to break this strong hold of satan on our nation. I pray that the United States is not simply one of the other nations of the world that reject GOD in the end times. I hope our leaders will wake up from spiritual sleep.

**"The grass withers and the flowers fade,
But the word of our GOD stands forever."
(ISAIAH 40:8)**

The United States of America has factually been one of Israel's most faithful allies, and GOD'S promise to Abraham, "I will bless those who bless you" (Genesis 12:3a), has resulted in America's success. If not, the answer will be yes if America rejects and crosses GOD'S own boundary. We as a nation will bear the consequences if we do. But if America turns its back on Israel, it will lose GOD'S favor: "Whoever curses you I will curse" (Genesis 12:3b). GOD is not respecter of persons, including the world superpower.

"The grass withers and the flowers fade,
But the word of our GOD stands forever."
(ISAIAH 40:8)

CHAPTER 16

CONCLUSION

In conclusion, the Pursuit of Holiness is not just for individuals but for the entire nation. "Fear of GOD is the beginning of wisdom." A fool has said in his heart that there is no GOD. We live in an unprecedented time, and Biblical prophecy is unfolding before our very eyes. JESUS-YESHUA told us to be looking at Israel and the nations of the earth and how they treat the Jewish people. Strongly believe that the pursuit of holiness is a combined undertaking concerning GOD and the Christian. No one individual can achieve any mark of holiness short of GOD working in his or her life, nonetheless just as with conviction no one will reach holiness without determination on his or her own part.

When we allow the indwell of the Holy Spirit in our lives, HE continually makes us to be aware of our need for holiness; even as we grow in it. In addition, also the devil tries to use this effort of mindfulness of the HOLY SPIRIT to dishearten us, nonetheless we can often check our redemption in CHRIST'S righteousness in addition to be fortified. He makes us see CHRIST as our case in point in the direction of pleasing and doing the will of GOD. It is only the HOLY SPIRIT of GOD that strengthens us in our personal role in our pursuit of holiness. It is through acquaintance to the SORD OF THE SPIRIT which is the WORD OF GOD; and their applications in our everyday living will help us to be holy to our GOD. I believe also that memorizing the Bible is an effective way to affect our minds in living a holy live.

My belief is that there is likelihood of us failing in our pursuit of holiness, therefore our requirement for discipline is to achieve holiness. My brothers and sisters' chastisement starts with the Bible, so the need for an organized time for hearing, reading, studying, memorizing, and meditating on the WORD of GOD. There is doubt that reading the WORD of GOD provides us the overall viewpoint of heavenly truth, while reading of a passage or topic allows us to excavate more intensely into a fact. Memorizing the WORD of GOD will help us remember significant truths so applying them in our lives. We are meditating daily on the Scriptures to reflect about them, storing them in our hearts, and applying them to our life's situations.

> **"The grass withers and the flowers fade,**
> **But the word of our GOD stands forever."**
> **(ISAIAH 40:8)**

As we engage in the study of the Scripture, we must ask ourselves; what is it that GOD is teaching me here. What is my takeaway in this part of the Scripture that I studied? Friends Bible is not an ordinary Book! It is indispensable WORD of GOD! How does individual live a holy live affects their relationship with GOD? What does this passage teach me about GOD'S will for a holy life? The HOLY SPIRIT of GOD will surely teach us. HOLY SPIRIT is our helper. JESUS said in John 14:16; "And I will pray the Father, and He will give you another Helper, that He may abide with you forever" (John 14:16 NKJV). We also need to ask ourselves how does my life amount up to that Scripture; precisely where and how have I falling short of GOD's expectation? What indisputable stages of action do I need to take as the Scripture required me to do? Brethren, if we prosper in our pursuit of holiness we must persist even in our disappointments.

Our pursuit of holiness comprises the ability to control our physiques. There is a need to be steady in contradiction of laziness and excess in food and drinks. The fact is that as we give in to physical indolence, we are making room for spiritual laziness also. We need to be aware that laziness comes in many forms as a child of GOD. At times, we want to pray that it is the time the enemy of our soul will bring unwanted sleep. When it is time to go to prayer meetings the enemy will bring one excuse or the other for us not to go. If we cannot restrain ourselves from an indulgent appetite, you can be sure that it also be difficult to say no to lustful thoughts which include materialism which is the love of money, loss of flesh, think about the negative effects it has on us. Decreasing exposure to enticement would aid us in controlling our mistaken desires.

We are encouraged to run away from temptation and take constructive steps to evade it, and we are to circumvent thinking in what way to gratify our evil desires. There are requirements to study our wicked desires in addition to how they come about, to positively combat and dodge the exposure to evil attractions that activate them. However, we will be unsuccessful numerous times to keep our needs in check, by way for us to be contingent on the HOLY SPIRIT and continue, we can achieve the point of being intelligent to say not at all to those needs.

Brothers and sisters, living a holy life is not only a chastising the body then again also in needing a good thought life and soul. There is a possibility of being able to bodily confine ourselves to evil but however take part in such evil via the intentions of our minds. Holiness begins with our thoughts and works out to our movements. We are encouraged to always protect what we feed our minds through social media, TV, movies, music, etc., all these affect our minds. It is imperative for us to look at Philippians 4:8 as a standard for filtering what

"The grass withers and the flowers fade,
But the word of our GOD stands forever."
(ISAIAH 40:8)

we feed our minds. Part of Apostle Paul's letter to the brethren in Philippian he wrote, "Finally, brethren, whatever things are true, whatever things are noble, whatever things are just, whatever things are pure, whatever things are lovely, whatever things are of good report, if there is any virtue and if there is anything praiseworthy meditate on these things" (Philippians 4:8 NKJV).

In as much as we try to get out of being tempted, we ourselves must guarantee that we should not cause enticement to others. There are sins which defile the mind, for instance, envy, bitterness, being critical, retaliatory spirit, hatred, and jealousy. We need to do everything to get rid of them with the help of HOLY SPIRIT. I strongly encourage all of us to call on our HEAVENLY FATHER in prayer for humbleness to truthfully see our sins, and the grace and mercy to substitute them with pleasing thoughts.

The 1st episode of Apostle demands that all CHRIST followers to live a life of holiness 1st Peter 1:13-25). Truthfully, holy living means that Belivers should live a life that is set apart, held in reserve to give glory to GOD. It is a life of self-control, dedication, and care to essentials of righteous living. When we faithfully obey JESUS CHRIST, it means that we are living a holy life as we are required by GOD HIMSELF. GOD'S primary attribute is Holiness. It is not debatable or negotiable. Even though the WORD of GOD declares that GOD is love and GOD is merciful, the one and only attribute of GOD is repetitive three times. The Prophet Isaiah noted that "In a great chorus they sang, "holy, holy, holy is the LORD Almighty! The whole earth is filled with his glory!" (Isaiah 6:3 NLT). "Thus, I will make known my holy name among my people of Israel, I will not let it be desecrated anymore. And the nations too, will know that I am the LORD, the Holy One of Israel" (Ezekiel 39:7 NLT).

**"The grass withers and the flowers fade,
But the word of our GOD stands forever."
(ISAIAH 40:8)**

As the title of this book says, "Pursuit of Holiness," You might ask, "Why should I pursue holiness?" instead of pursuit of happiness? In the first place, every one of us believers

should pursue holy living because of appreciation for all JESUS CHRIST has done for us HIS followers. Once we are truthfully overcome through the price CHRIST paid to redeem us and saved us out of our sinful lifestyle, why should we ever want to go back? Our love for GOD should be our motivating factor in living a holy live. Jesus said, "If you keep My commandments, you will abide in My love, just as I have kept My Father's commandments and abide in His love" (John 15.10 NKJV). Loving Jesus leads you to holy living.

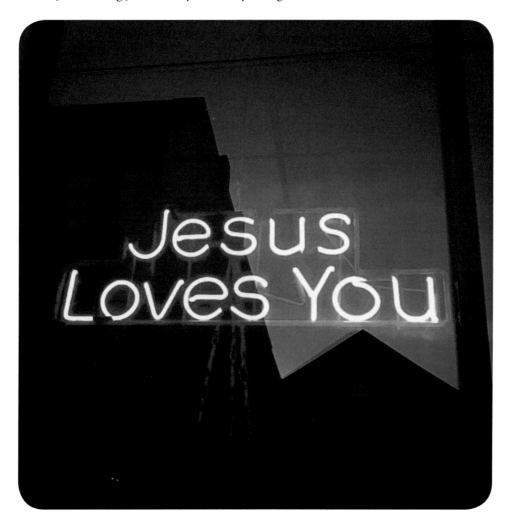

Surrender your life today to JESUS CHRIST. Tomorrow might be too late for you. There is no repentance in the grave. Today is your day; so, maximize the moment with JESUS CHRIST YOUR SAVIOR. HE LOVES YOU SO MUCH. He saved me and HE is willing to save you and make you a new creature in HIM.

Thank you for taking time out to read this book hope it has encouraged you to aspire to live a holy life as required by GOD and may the LORD bless you richly.

"The grass withers and the flowers fade,
But the word of our GOD stands forever."
(ISAIAH 40:8)

ABOUT THE AUTHOR

Dorothy came from a polygamous family. She loves the LORD. Accept CHRIST AS HER LORD and SAVIOR in November of 1974. She is very enthusiastic about missions. She has been to Burundi in Central Africa, Ecuador in South America, and Nigeria in West Africa multiple times.

Dorothy worked as a medical director for African Christian Fellowship Midwest Region for four years. She worked as children and youth director for 6 years. She also served in African Christian Fellowship USA as the youth and young adult over 10 years as the councilor. Was the Secretary for two terms in African Christian Fellowship Chicago North?

She has been a professional Registered Nurse for over 30 years. She is Executive Director and Founder of New Hope HIV/AIDS Education and Prevention (A USA based non-profit organization). She is a business consultant, a motivational speaker, an encourager, and a prayer warrior. She is currently the Program Coordinator for Women of Divine Purpose; a women's prayer group based in Chicago, Illinois. She is a member of Wailing Women Worldwide.

Mrs. Princewill has been married to the husband of her youth for 44 years. She has three grown sons. Two GOD-given daughters. Have many grandchildren and thirteen GOD Children. A member of Assembly of GOD Church since her conversion and have served in different roles of the Church.

Printed in the United States
by Baker & Taylor Publisher Services